Pioneer Days in the Wyoming Valley

Also from Westphalia Press
westphaliapress.org

The Idea of the Digital University

Bulwarks Against Poverty in America

Treasures of London

Avate Garde Politician

L'Enfant and the Freemasons

Baronial Bedrooms

Making Trouble for Muslims

Philippine Masonic Directory ~ 1918

Paddle Your Own Canoe

Opportunity and Horatio Alger

Careers in the Face of Challenge

Bookplates of the Kings

Hymns to the Gods

Freemasonry in Old Buffalo

Original Cables from the Pearl Harbor Attack

Social Satire and the Modern Novel

The Essence of Harvard

The Genius of Freemasonry

A Definitive Commentary on Bookplates

James Martineau and Rebuilding Theology

Bohemian San Francisco

The Wizard

Crime 3.0

Anti-Masonry and the Murder of Morgan

Understanding Art

Spies I Knew

Lodge "Himalayan Brotherhood" No. 459 C.E.

Ancient Masonic Mysteries

Collecting Old Books

Masonic Secret Signs and Passwords

Death Valley in '49

Lariats and Lassos

Mr. Garfield of Ohio

The Wisdom of Thomas Starr King

The French Foreign Legion

War in Syria

Naturism Comes to the United States

New Sources on Women and Freemasonry

Designing, Adapting, Strategizing in Online Education

Gunboat and Gun-runner

Memoirs of a Poor Relation

Espionage!

Bohemian San Francisco

Tales of Old Japan

Pioneer Days in the Wyoming Valley

by Mary Hinchcliffe Joyce

WESTPHALIA PRESS
An imprint of Policy Studies Organization

Pioneer Days in the Wyoming Valley
All Rights Reserved © 2016 by Policy Studies Organization

Westphalia Press
An imprint of Policy Studies Organization
1527 New Hampshire Ave., NW
Washington, D.C. 20036
info@ipsonet.org

ISBN-13: 978-1-63391-389-9
ISBN-10: 1-63391-389-9

Cover design by Taillefer Long at Illuminated Stories:
www.illuminatedstories.com

Daniel Gutierrez-Sandoval, Executive Director
PSO and Westphalia Press

Updated material and comments on this edition
can be found at the Westphalia Press website:
www.westphaliapress.org

DARLEY'S WYOMING

To

My Mother and the Memory
of My Father and the Pioneer Mothers
and Fathers of the Wyoming Valley

This Book Is Dedicated

PIONEER DAYS
IN THE
WYOMING VALLEY

by

MARY HINCHCLIFFE JOYCE

CONTENTS

I	Early History of the Wyoming Valley...	15
II	Visit of the First White Man..........	26
III	First White Settlement in the Wyoming Valley, 1762. Massacre of 1763......	32
IV	Proprietaries Begin Settlement of Wyoming Valley	41
V	Capture of Fort Durkee by Yankees.....	51
VI	The Events of 1771..................	58
VII	Important Meeting of the Susquehanna Company at Hartford	68
VIII	Plans Made by Settlers for Protection of Wyoming Valley	78
IX	Death of the Hardings and Hadsalls.....	86
X	The Story of Frances Slocum.........	99
XI	Controversy Between Pennsylvania and Connecticut Begins Anew	105
XII	The End of the Story................	117
	Index	119

LIST OF ILLUSTRATIONS

	PAGE
DARLEY'S WYOMING	*Frontispiece*
COUNT ZINZENDORF	20
PENN'S TREATY WITH THE INDIANS	28
COVERED WAGON	32
TEEDYUSCUNG	36
BURNING OF WYOMING	44
HON. JOHN WILKES	48
COL. ISAAC BARRE	52
BLOCKHOUSE	60
WYOMING FORT	64
MORTAR AND PESTLE	68
MYERS HOUSE	76
FORTY-FORT	80
CAPITULATION TABLE	84
TABLET	92
WYOMING MONUMENT	96
FRANCES SLOCUM	100
GEN. JOHN SULLIVAN	108
CHEVALIER DE LA LUZERNE	112
EARLY MAP OF WYOMING	116

PREFACE

This book was written at the request of my husband, who has many times expressed regret over the fact that up to this time a history of the Wyoming Valley has not been available for children.

And so I have tried to tell the story of Pioneer Days in the Wyoming Valley in a way that will appeal to children and grown-ups alike.

In preparing the manuscript, the following authorities were consulted: *History of Wyoming*, by Isaac A. Chapman, Esq.; Honorable Charles Miner's *History of Wyoming;* Sherman Day's *History of Pennsylvania; The Pennsylvania Archives* and the *Frontier Forts of Pennsylvania*. To all of them I am deeply grateful for the help they have given me.

The cuts of the pictures have been loaned me by the Wyoming Historical and Geological Society, and I want to extend thanks to that organization. Without the pictures my book would not be complete.

I also want to express my appreciation of the co-operation of Miss Frances Dorrance, Director of the Wyoming Historical and Geological Society. To Miss Dorrance I am grateful for advice and criticism which have meant so much to me in completing the book.

To the coming Sesqui-Centennial, I am indebted for the additional incentive to finish the book as soon as possible.

And last, but not least, I am deeply grateful to my husband, my children and the children of the Wyoming Valley for inspiring me to write this book.

Pittston, Pa.
June 30, 1928.

PIONEER DAYS IN THE
WYOMING VALLEY

I
EARLY HISTORY OF THE WYOMING VALLEY

ONE rainy day during the month of January, 1928, the children were gathered around the fireplace telling stories. Outside the wind howled, and the raindrops beat against the window-panes as if they would like to join the happy circle. Grandmother had tired of her knitting, and sat smiling at the sunny faces before her.

When the children had finished telling their stories, it was Grandmother's turn, and they all crowded around her chair. "A story, Grandmother!" they cried.

"Oh! tell us something about the Wyoming Valley," George pleaded. "You know, Grandmother, you promised to tell us something about the Wyoming Massacre before the celebration."

At this time the people of the Wyoming Valley were just beginning to make plans for the Sesqui-Centennial, as July 3, 1928, would be the one hundred and fiftieth (150th) anniversary of the Battle of Wyoming.

Grandmother put aside her knitting, adjusted her spectacles, and, after looking over her prospective audience, her eyes glowing with happiness, began.

"Before I tell you anything about the Wyoming Valley, you must first get your geographies and turn to the map of Pennsylvania." The children scurried away, and were soon back with their books. The map found, they waited expectantly.

"How many of you can find Luzerne County?" asked Grandmother. All the children except little Frances raised their hands. "Now follow the mountain ranges that run through the County east and west of the Susquehanna River. Can you tell me what you find nestling at the bases of these mountains?"

"I know," answered Joe. "It is a valley, because it is a tract of land lying between mountains."

"Well, my dear, you are right," answered Grandmother, "and I want you to look at it carefully, because between these two mountain ranges lies the beautiful Wyoming Valley that we all love so much.

"You know, children," continued Grandmother, "whenever I speak of the Wyoming Valley it brings back to me a few lines of a poem I read when I was a little girl, and these are the words that I have never forgotten.

> Home's not merely four square walls,
>   Though with pictures hung and gilded,
> Home is where affection calls,
>   Filled with shrines the heart hath builded.

"I apologize to the writer if my quotation is not correctly worded," continued Grandmother, "but these words run through my mind many times, and I think of them again today because the Wyoming Valley has always been my home just as it has been yours, and for me it is filled with many shrines the heart hath builded.

Now, children, I know you are anxious to hear the story of the Wyoming Massacre, but you will have to

HISTORY OF WYOMING VALLEY 17

be patient and first learn something about the earlier history of the valley.

Many years ago before the coming of the white man to Wyoming there dwelt on the banks of the Susquehanna River a race of people called Indians or redskins. Chapman, a local historian of early days, tells us that when the white settlers first arrived in the Wyoming Valley they found the remains of ancient fortifications. The people who had built them had left the valley long before the Indians arrived here, and their origin is shrouded in mystery. We do not know where those people came from, how long they remained here, or where they went. All we know about them is that they left fortifications in the valley that were entirely different from what the Indians would build.

Our knowledge of the history of the Wyoming Valley begins with the eighteenth century, and the earliest known inhabitants, the Indians.

GRANDMOTHER DESCRIBES THE INDIANS

I suppose you would all like to know something about the first inhabitants of the valley. The Indians had reddish colored skin, and that is why the white men called them redskins. They had high cheek bones, their eyes were black and their hair straight, black and coarse.

Their weapons and tools were made of stone and animal bones, and even today farmers along the river in the valley plow up arrowheads made of stone.

Their clothes were not made of cloth like those you wear today, but of deerskins sewed together with the sinews of the deer or other animals. Moccasins also made of skins were used instead of shoes.

The men of the tribes hunted and fished. They cultivated the land between the tree stumps by scratching the ground with a stone, a piece of flat, sharp bone or a pointed stick. Here they planted corn and beans and sometimes pumpkins. The beans were planted in the hills with the corn and grew up the cornstalks instead of on poles as we grow them. When the beans and corn were ready to eat, the Indians cooked them together, and they called this dish "succotash," just as we do today. When the corn was ripe in the fall, they pounded it between two stones into a coarse meal, which they mixed with water and made into cakes.

Now before coming to America the white settlers did not know anything of these good foods, and just think, children, if the white men had not found the Indians growing corn, beans and pumpkins you probably would never have tasted Johnny cake, pumpkin pie or succotash.

We are told that sometimes the Indians would dig a hole and line it with smooth stones. They would then build a fire in the hole, and keep it burning until the stones were very hot. When they were hot enough they would pull out the ashes, and place corn, game or fish in the hole. You see, even the Indians had their fireless cookers, and they no doubt found this a very good way to cook their food.

I almost forgot to tell you about the little Indian boys and girls. The Indian baby was called a papoose. He was not cuddled as you children have been, and he had no bassinet or crib. Instead of being placed in a warm bed and covered up with blankets, he was strapped to a board which was usually lined with some animal skin, the soft fur side being placed next the baby's body. As the mother was almost always busy this board was hung on the limb of a tree where it was swung and rocked by the wind. When the mother moved about from one place to another the board on which the baby was strapped hung from her back.

When he was able to run about he did not have toys, but helped his mother. Then as he grew older he learned to swim and run, and he also learned to make and use a bow and arrow. He learned to trap animals. Later he was taught how to hunt and fight. We are told he was not considered a man until he had killed an enemy and taken his scalp.

The life of a little Indian girl was much the same, but she was taught to sew, cook and cultivate the ground. The women no doubt did most of the scratching of the soil and the planting as the men were almost always engaged in hunting and fishing.

INDIAN TRIBES WHO DWELT IN THE WYOMING VALLEY

The Indians who dwelt in the Wyoming Valley were divided into three tribes, the Shawnees, Delawares and Nanticokes. They did not own the land on which they lived, as they had emigrated from other parts of the country and settled here.

The whole Wyoming Valley was claimed by the Iroquois or Six Nations, a confederacy or union (like our United States) of powerful tribes who lived in central New York State. The Indians in the valley just had the right to live here, as you children would have the right to live in a house you had leased from the owner.

Now, how many of you would like to hear more about the Indians who lived in the Wyoming Valley?

"Oh, Grandmother, please tell us more about them," begged Mary Patricia. "We all want to hear more about them, even Frances. Don't you, dear?"

"Yes, Grandmother, and do you think there are any

Indians around here now?" answered that little four-year-old darling.

Grandmother looked around at her interested circle before she replied. "No, dear, the Indians live far away from the Wyoming Valley now, and if you are all very good I will tell you how they first came to settle in the valley."

THE SHAWNEES

The Shawnees were the first tribe of Indians to settle here. Their home was away down in the southeastern part of the United States, in Georgia and Florida. They were a ferocious tribe who were never satisfied unless they were fighting with their neighbors, and this made all the Indians who lived near them very unhappy. After putting up with this condition for a long time the neighboring tribes got together and drove them out of their homeland.

This left the Shawnees without a home, and the whole tribe moved north looking for a place to settle. They had heard of the Delaware tribe whose language was very much like their own. A messenger was sent to the Delaware chief asking permission to settle in his territory under the protection of the Delawares. Now the land on which the Delawares were located was claimed by the Six Nations, and the Delaware braves thought it would be a good thing to have the Shawnees to help them if trouble arose with those powerful tribes. They accordingly gave them a tract of land on which to settle.

The Shawnees, like many people today, were very ungrateful, and soon began to quarrel with their benefactors. This continued for some time, and the Dela-

COUNT ZINZENDORF

HISTORY OF WYOMING VALLEY 21

wares finally forced the Shawnees to vacate their settlement.

Once more homeless the Shawnees wandered about looking for a place to settle where they could have a good supply of food and water. They finally located a site in the lower end of the Wyoming Valley. Here they built a settlement which they called Shawnee. This town was situated on the west bank of the Susquehanna near what is now Plymouth. This was the first Indian settlement in the Wyoming Valley. The early name for Plymouth was "Shawnee," and this is also the Indian name for Harvey's Lake.

THE DELAWARES. TROUBLE OVER BOUNDARIES. CONFERENCE AT PHILADELPHIA. DELAWARES ORDERED OUT OF THEIR TERRITORY BY THE SIX NATIONS. MOVE TO WYOMING VALLEY. TROUBLE WITH THE SHAWNEES. BATTLE FOUGHT. SHAWNEES LEAVE VALLEY.

Now while the Shawnee tribe was enjoying peace on the banks of the Susquehanna the Delawares were again in trouble in their settlement on the Delaware. This time the trouble was not with another tribe of Indians, but with the people then governing the lands granted to William Penn, who were known as the Proprietaries of Pennsylvania. The Delawares had sold some land to the Proprietaries, but when the time came to turn the purchase over to the new owners, they refused to keep their part of the contract, giving as a reason that the boundaries were not satisfactory.

Unable to come to an agreement with the Delawares the governor sent a messenger to the chiefs of the Six Nations asking them to send deputies to attend a conference to be held in Philadelphia.

This conference was held during the summer of

1742 in the Great Hall of the Council House in Philadelphia. Two hundred and thirty Indians represented the Six Nations. The chiefs of the Delawares were also present together with officers of the Colonial Government and many private citizens.

The governor opened the conference and explained that the Proprietaries had bought the land from the Delawares, and had paid the price agreed on. He also produced the papers relating to the transaction. The representatives of the Six Nations were very cross at the Delawares for not keeping faith with the white men and ordered them to leave the settlement at once. They were given a choice of two places to locate in, Wyoming or Shamokin.

The Delawares moved at once and part of the tribe took up their residence in Wyoming.

On arriving in the valley they found the Shawnees there before them. You will remember the Shawnees were living on the west bank of the river, and so the Delawares selected the east bank for their settlement. Here they built a town which they called Maughwauwame. Historians tell us that the word means great or large plains. They also tell us that many years later when the white men came to the valley they found the word hard to pronounce and called the Indian village "Wauwaumie," "Wiwaumic," "Wiomic," and finally "Wyoming."

So you see, children, an important thing to remember is that the Wyoming Valley takes its name from the Indian town of "Maughwauwame" built by the Delawares in the lower part of the valley during the summer of 1742.

A bitter feeling still existed between the Delawares and Shawnees, and many quarrels arose between them. This went on for some time until one day, as Chapman tells us, several Shawnee squaws and their chil-

HISTORY OF WYOMING VALLEY 23

dren crossed the river in canoes and began to pick wild fruits that grew along the river bank below Maughwauwame. The Delaware squaws, also in search of fruits, came upon the Shawnees, and they were indignant when they found their enemies encroaching on what they considered their domain. While the women were busy picking, one of the Shawnee children caught a large grasshopper. The Delaware children wanted it and a fight started. Soon all the women and children on both sides were fighting. Stones were no doubt used as weapons as some of both tribes were killed. The Shawnees were driven down the bank to their canoes, and hurriedly pushed across the river to their own settlement. The braves of the tribes were out hunting game, and upon returning home at once made ready to avenge the deaths of their loved ones.

The Shawnee warriors crossed the river in canoes, but the Delawares were waiting for them and would not let them land. A great many of the braves were killed before the Shawnees succeeded in gaining the shore. Then their meeting with the Delawares proved disastrous, as only about one-half of their number survived the battle that was fought. These returned to their canoes and crossed the river to Shawnee. A short time later what was left of the tribe removed to the Ohio.

NANTICOKES SETTLE IN VALLEY

In 1748 the Nanticokes, another tribe of Indians related to the Delawares and coming from Chesapeake Bay, arrived in Wyoming and located in the lower end of the valley. They were a peaceful tribe who had been driven out of their own territory by the coming of the white settlers. They remained in the valley about seven years and then moved farther north.

"Now, children," said Grandmother, "I have told you what I know of the earliest settlements in the Wyoming Valley. I hope you have all paid strict attention, because tomorrow I am going to ask you some questions about the Indians who lived here many years ago."

SECOND DAY OF GRANDMOTHER'S STORY

The next day was clear and cold. The rain had turned into snow, but even the joys of sleigh riding were forgotten by the children, and Grandmother found her audience awaiting her in the living-room. They had hurried home from school, and were soon busy answering the questions Grandmother asked.

See how many of them you can answer before you go on with the story.

LIST OF QUESTIONS

Where is the Wyoming Valley situated?
When does the history of the valley begin?
Who were the earliest known inhabitants?
Describe them.
How many tribes of Indians dwelt in the Wyoming Valley?
Name them.
Were they natives of the valley?
Tell me something about the Shawnees.
Where was the first Indian settlement in the Wyoming Valley located, and what was it called?
Where did the Delawares come from?
Why did they leave their settlement?
What Indian town did they build in the Wyoming Valley?

HISTORY OF WYOMING VALLEY 25

What is the origin of the name "Wyoming"?

Tell in your own words the story of the trouble between the Delawares and Shawnees.

When did the Nanticokes settle in the Wyoming Valley?

How long did they remain here?

"Well, children," continued Grandmother, "you have done very well, and I am going to tell you a little of the history of the valley each day, and the following day I will ask you questions about what I have told you. So pay strict attention to my story. Every little boy and girl in Luzerne County should know something of the history of the Wyoming Valley, and I want you to come here every day right after school. How many of you can I depend on?" Every hand was raised and Grandmother, much pleased with the interest shown by her audience, went on with the story.

II

VISIT OF THE FIRST WHITE MAN

"Now, children, we must go back again to 1742, the year the Delawares took up their residence in the Wyoming Valley. We are told that it was during this same year that the first white man visited the valley. This man was Count Nicholas L. Zinzendorf who had traveled all the way from Saxony to preach to the Indians the doctrine of the Moravian church, which is one of the many Christian churches. For this purpose, he came up the Susquehanna to Shamokin (now Sunbury), and then up to the Wyoming Valley, entering it from the South, and put up his tent a little below the town of Shawnee.

Upon learning of his presence in the neighborhood the Indians became alarmed and decided to kill him. Under cover of darkness the plotters approached the tent silently so that not a sound reached his ears. The unsuspecting missionary was all alone busily engaged with some papers on which we are told he was writing. The night was cold and he had built a fire which soon warmed up his tent. A rattlesnake attracted by the heat crawled into the shelter and passed over Count Zinzendorf's legs without disturbing or harming him.

It was just at this time that the Indians looked in upon their intended victim, who was unaware of the snake's presence. The sight that met their gaze filled their hearts with fear. One glance was enough. They hurriedly left the scene, and on reaching the town told their friends that Count Zinzendorf was under the pro-

THE FIRST WHITE MAN 27

tection of the Great Spirit, since even a rattlesnake would not attempt to harm him. The Indians who had been so anxious to put the Count to death now became his friends, and many of them were converted to the Moravian faith. Count Zinzendorf remained in the valley for some time and established a mission here. He then returned to Bethlehem, the Pennsylvania home of the Moravians.

CONNECTICUT'S CLAIM TO THE WYOMING VALLEY. WILLIAM PENN'S CLAIM TO THE WYOMING VALLEY. OVERLAPPING OF CLAIMS CAUSE OF PENNAMITE-YANKEE WAR

Now if you will again take up your geographies, and turn to the map of the United States, you will find that in order to reach Connecticut today you must travel over part of the State of New York. It will no doubt surprise you to learn that the Wyoming Valley was at one time a part of the Connecticut Colony. This is how it happened.

Connecticut was first settled by the Puritans in 1634-35. They were natives of England and like the Pilgrims were seeking a home where they would be free from religious persecution. They did not have a charter for their colony, which worried them very much, and so in 1660 they petitioned the king for a confirmation of their right to Connecticut. A charter was granted to the Connecticut Colony by Charles II. in 1662, in which the South Sea or Pacific Ocean was named as the western boundary. The Wyoming Valley was included in the grant covered by this charter.

So you see Connecticut's claim to the Wyoming Valley was established as early as 1662 through the charter granted to the Connecticut Colony by Charles II.

Nineteen years later, in 1681, this same king, Charles II., granted another charter, this time to William Penn, the founder of Pennsylvania, and the territory covered by this charter also included the Wyoming Valley. Now pay attention while I tell you how this came about.

William Penn was an Englishman and a son of Admiral Penn to whom Charles II. owed a debt of sixteen thousand pounds sterling. Now, when Admiral Penn died, his son William inherited all his property, which included the money owed him by Charles II. William Penn was a Quaker, and he was anxious to establish a colony in America where his people would be free from persecution. So he went to King Charles II. and suggested that he give him a tract of land in America instead of the money he owed him. Charles was delighted as this was an easy way for him to pay the debt. So in 1681 he made the grant of all the land included in the present State of Pennsylvania to William Penn. The Wyoming Valley, as you know, was included in this grant.

From the story I have just told you, you will understand why the Wyoming Valley was claimed by two colonies. The Connecticut colony claimed our valley under the Connecticut charter, and the Proprietaries of Pennsylvania based their claim on the grant made to William Penn.

Almost a century later this overlapping of claims led to a controversy between the Connecticut colony and the Proprietaries of Pennsylvania which lasted for many years, and is known as the Pennamite-Yankee Wars.

And unconscious of the coming storm, the Wyoming Valley, with her great mineral wealth and productive soil, smilingly awaited the coming of the white man to shower him with her lavish gifts.

PENN'S TREATY WITH THE INDIANS

THE FIRST WHITE MAN 29

BEGINNING OF FRENCH AND INDIAN WAR. TREATY WITH INDIANS. BRADDOCK'S DEFEAT. INDIANS ALLY THEMSELVES WITH FRENCH ARMY. GENERAL COUNCIL HELD AT EASTON

We will now pass over a period of seventy-three years to July 3, 1754, when the first battle of the French and Indian War was fought. In this battle George Washington, at the head of a small force, was defeated by the French commander. You may wonder why I speak of this battle, and how it could have any bearing on conditions in the Wyoming Valley.

Well, when the French defeated the English colonists many of the Indians were so impressed by the French victory that they allied themselves with the French army, and became enemies of the English. This did not please the English, and they were very much alarmed. So the governors of the colonies tried to renew their friendship with the Indians. A general congress was held at Albany. Many Indians attended this congress, and were met by committees from the English settlements. The result was that the Indians agreed to live in peace and friendship with the English.

About a year later, in 1755, the British regulars under General Braddock were defeated by the French and Indians about ten miles from Fort DuQuesne, now Pittsburgh. General Braddock was killed together with a large number of his troops. Washington rallied the survivors and led them to safety. As a result of this battle a number of the Indian tribes again allied themselves with the French army.

The English now became alarmed in earnest, and in an effort to get back the friendship of the Indians, invited them to a general conference at Easton. This conference was held in Easton in July, 1756, and proved a failure, the attendance being poor. The

English, although no doubt discouraged at the failure of the conference, did not give up hope for a reconciliation, and arrangements were made to hold a general council at Easton in November.

On November 8, 1756, the chiefs and representatives of the Indian tribes met the governor and his party in general council at Easton. This conference lasted for a period of nine days. All complaints were talked over and settled. As a result of this conference a treaty of peace was made by the English with the Delawares and Shawnees.

The English were now anxious to secure a peace pledge from the Six Nations who were so powerful they were feared by English and Indians alike. But it was not until two years later in October, 1758, that a grand council of all the Indian tribes was held at Easton. About five hundred Indian chiefs and deputies were present and Pennsylvania and New Jersey were represented by a large number of leading citizens.

This conference lasted eighteen days, and all the differences existing between the English and Indians were adjusted. On the 26th day of October, 1758, a treaty of peace was signed. This treaty was kept until October, 1763, when hostilities again broke out with a terrible massacre of the first settlers in the Wyoming Valley, which I will tell you about later.

THIRD DAY

The second day Grandmother had told the children about the first white man who visited the Wyoming Valley. She also explained the reason why the Wyoming Valley was claimed by two colonies. A review of these chapters will help you to a better understanding of later developments.

THE FIRST WHITE MAN 31

QUESTIONS

Who was the first white man to visit the Wyoming Valley?

Tell the story of his visit.

On what charter did the Connecticut colonists base their claim to the Wyoming Valley?

When was this charter granted, and by whom?

Did William Penn also claim the Wyoming Valley?

What territory was included in the grant made by Charles II to William Penn?

Tell the story of this grant.

What was the cause of the Pennamite-Yankee wars?

What bearing did the French and Indian War have on conditions in the Wyoming Valley?

Why did the English hold a General Congress at Albany in 1754?

What was accomplished by this Congress?

Was the conference held in Easton in July, 1756, a success?

Where was the third meeting held? How long did it last?

What was the result?

When and where was the fourth conference held?

How many Indians were present?

What English colonies were represented?

How long did this conference last?

When was the Treaty of Peace signed, and how long was it kept?

III

FIRST WHITE SETTLEMENT IN THE WYOMING VALLEY IN 1762. MASSACRE OF 1763

Now, children, we are coming to the part of the story that will no doubt interest you most. So far I have introduced to you people and events that have a part in this story.

For more than a century the Connecticut colony had been growing in size, and many small towns had sprung up throughout the territory covered by the Connecticut charter. The towns were no doubt becoming crowded, and a number of the colonists decided to seek new homes in the wilderness. Scouts from these settlements had brought back stories of the beauty and fertility of the Wyoming Valley—of its fish and game and farming lands.

So, on July 18, 1753, several hundred people, who were members of the Connecticut colony, met at Windham, Connecticut, and formed an association called the Susquehanna Company. The object of this company was the establishing of a settlement on the banks of the Susquehanna River.

At this meeting seven men were appointed to visit the territory along the Susquehanna, to see if it would be a good place to start a new settlement. If satisfactory, they were instructed to buy the land from the Indians who claimed it, and to survey and lay out the district they thought suitable for the founding of a new settlement.

COVERED WAGON

FIRST WHITE SETTLEMENT 33

In order to pay the expenses of the committee, each member of the association pledged himself to pay to a properly appointed treasurer for the company "Two Spanish Milled Dollars." This money was to be paid before the committee appointed started out on their journey.

Before going on with my story, I think I had better explain to you the meaning of a "Spanish Milled Dollar." This coin, according to the *National Encyclopedia,* was first minted at Joachimsthal in 1519. It was an old German coin minted from Bohemian silver. It was known as the Joachimsthaler or Thaler, for short, and "was for a time the European standard of weight and purity." From the word "Thaler," our word "dollar" comes. Later the name was adopted by Spain and her colonies, and through trade with the West Indies the American colonists began to use this Spanish Milled Dollar. When a system of coinage was established by Congress in 1792, "the basis was made a dollar 'of the value of a Spanish Milled Dollar.'"

The name "milled" comes from the grooves you find around the edges of silver and gold coins. This milling prevents a dishonest person from paring away any of the valuable metal.

Well, the seven men appointed set out on their long journey through the wilderness. They no doubt followed the Indian paths whenever possible as there were no roads in those days. And, after enduring the many inconveniences and hardships occasioned by such a trip, they at last found themselves on the banks of the Susquehanna River.

After satisfying themselves that the valley along the Susquehanna would be a good location in which to plant a new colony, they again started out on another long journey. This time their footsteps pointed toward

Albany, where, you will remember, the English and Indians held a peace congress in 1754. The object of this visit to Albany was to buy from the Six Nations their title to the lands along the Susquehanna. The Indians sold them the territory they desired, and this deal is known as the "Susquehanna Purchase."[1] This is how the Susquehanna Company secured the Indian title to the Wyoming Valley. Of course, it was not known as the Wyoming Valley until some years later.

Nothing further was done until the following year, 1755. In May of that year a meeting of the Susquehanna Company was held at Hartford, at which a committee was appointed to meet with the Indians and erect monuments at the northeast and southeast corners of the land they had purchased from them. I suppose the object of this was to establish boundaries so that they would not have trouble later. The committee was also instructed to lay out townships, and was further given authority to admit settlers to this land.

For the protection and convenience of the people who would begin colonizing the Wyoming Valley, the company agreed to pay for the erection of a fortification, a gristmill and sawmill. These buildings were to be put up wherever the committee considered them "necessary for the encouragement and security of the first settlers."

The committee visited the valley, but their report on conditions here was evidently not satisfactory, as a settlement was not started for several years. This was the year of Braddock's defeat by the French, when many of the Indians allied themselves with the French army.

Some years later, on May 19, 1762, another important meeting of the Susquehanna Company was

---
[1] July 11, 1754.

FIRST WHITE SETTLEMENT 35

held at Hartford, when plans were made for one hundred members of the Susquehanna Company to proceed to the Susquehanna Purchase, and take possession of a tract of land ten miles square, east of the Susquehanna River, and improve same. This offer was good for four months, and any man taking advantage of it would have to live on his grant for a period of five years in order to secure a title to it.

Two months later, on July 27, 1762, a meeting was held at which the number of settlers and the size of the grant were increased. It was voted at this meeting that two hundred men proceed to the Susquehanna Purchase and begin the settlement of the valley on the same terms as laid down at the meeting of May 19th. And ten miles on the west side of the river, opposite the first grant, were set aside for the additional one hundred settlers. The time for starting the settlement was limited to three months from July 27th.

You will remember a treaty of peace had been signed by the English and Indians in 1758, and the Connecticut settlers, feeling that the Indians were now their friends, thought it a good time to settle the valley. And so, in the summer of 1762, about two hundred settlers left the security of their homes in Connecticut and traveled many weary miles through an almost pathless wilderness to establish a colony here in our Wyoming Valley.

After reaching the banks of the Susquehanna they began looking around for a location, and finally decided on a tract of land at the mouth of Mill Creek. As soon as they had selected the site for their settlement, they began to cut down trees from which they trimmed away the limbs, and soon log cabins began to spring up where a few days earlier trees were growing. These crude homes afforded the settlers a shelter from the elements and the wild beasts that lived in the surrounding forests.

Their next work was to cut the grass, uproot saplings, and dig out stones. After a few acres had been cleared, they began to cultivate the soil. Wheat was planted and the settlers were very busy until cold weather set in. Then they began to worry about food for the winter. Of course, they did not yet have a gristmill, and the nearest settlement was many miles away. The committee in charge of the little colony (John Jenkins, John Smith, and Stephen Gardner), were appealed to, and they advised the settlers to return to their homes in Connecticut for the winter. After concealing their tools and farming implements, they began the journey home.

The following year, 1763, found them again on their way to the Wyoming Valley. This time they were accompanied by their families. They also brought with them domestic animals, household goods and provisions. Great was their joy when, upon reaching Mill Creek, they found their possessions just as they had left them. They were soon settled in their homes of the previous year.

The Delaware Indians, who still retained their residence in the valley, were very friendly with their new neighbors. Their chief, a venerable man named Teedyuscung, was popular with the settlers and loved by all the members of his tribe, who, no doubt, resented the action of the Six Nations in selling their territory to the white men. Teedyuscung had always stood up for the rights of his people, and this made him doubly dear to all the members of his tribe. The Six Nations, on the other hand, disliked him as much as his own people loved him, and they must have watched his growing intimacy with the settlers with increasing hatred and unrest.

TEEDYUSCUNG

FIRST WHITE SETTLEMENT 37

In 1763 a number of warriors from the Six Nations made an apparently friendly visit to the settlement of the Delawares at Maughwauwame. One night, while Teedyuscung was asleep, the visitors set fire to his house. The building was consumed, and with it the poor old chieftain who was unable to get out. The guilty warriors pretended to sympathize with their hosts, and their attitude soon led the Delawares to believe that they were innocent of any wrongdoing. So they finally decided that the settlers were responsible for the death of their chief.

The inhabitants of the little colony, unaware of the bitter feeling stirred up by the action of the visiting warriors, went about their tasks with their hearts full of good will toward the Delawares. On the morning of October 15, 1763, they went to work in the fields as usual, without a thought of trouble with the Indians. In fact, they had journeyed to the valley without any means of defense, and were unprepared for an attack. Suddenly, without warning, the Delawares swooped down on them from all sides. About twenty of the defenseless settlers were killed. Several were taken prisoners. Those fortunate enough to escape gave the alarm, and a general exodus of the surviving colonists followed.

The Indians immediately took possession of the settlement. Domestic animals were seized and driven to Maughwauwame. The homes of the colonists were plundered. The savages then applied torches to the buildings. Soon the settlement was ablaze.

What a dreadful experience this must have been for those innocent people fleeing through the wilderness and looking back to see the homes, for which they had sacrificed so much, burning in the distance. Many of them hurried on through the forest, exposed to the chilly winds of October, insufficiently clad and

38 PIONEER DAYS IN WYOMING VALLEY

without food, their hearts torn by thoughts of husbands, fathers, and brothers left to the mercy of their fiendish captors.

What a contrast to the comfortable homes and conditions we enjoy in the valley today!

GOVERNOR OF PENNSYLVANIA ORDERS MILITIA TO DRIVE OUT INDIANS. DELAWARES ABANDON MAUGHWAUWAME. SOLDIERS BURY BODIES OF THE UNFORTUNATE SETTLERS.

The Governor of Pennsylvania, upon learning of the massacre, immediately ordered the militia to march to the Wyoming Valley and drive out the hostile natives. When the militia arrived at Wyoming, they found that the Indians had abandoned their settlement and left the valley. With them they had carried away the scalps of the dead settlers, also the men they had taken prisoners, and all movable plunder. The militia buried the bodies of the fallen settlers and then withdrew from the valley.

KING REFUSES TO ALLOW FURTHER SETTLEMENTS IN THE WYOMING VALLEY

The King of England, upon hearing of the terrible massacre, refused to allow any more entries on the Susquehanna Purchase until proper precautions had been taken to prevent further trouble with the Indians.

And so no further steps were taken to settle the Wyoming Valley for several years.

FOURTH DAY

The fourth day of the story was one that would tempt any child to stay outdoors, and Grandmother

FIRST WHITE SETTLEMENT 39

was agreeably surprised when she was greeted by a larger audience than on previous days. The children had brought along a few of their friends to hear the story. These are the questions she required the children to answer before she would take up the story again:

When and where was the Susquehanna Company formed?
What was the object of this company?
Tell what you know of the proceedings of the first meeting.
What is a "Spanish Milled Dollar"?
How many men were appointed to select a location for a settlement on the Susquehanna?
What was the "Susquehanna Purchase"?
What was done at the meeting of the Susquehanna Company held in May, 1755?
How many years elapsed before another important meeting was held?
What was done at that meeting?
What was the purpose of the meeting held in July, 1762?
When was the first settlement made in the Wyoming Valley?
How many colonists were there?
Where was the first settlement located?
Did the colonists remain in the valley during the winter of 1762?
Tell about their return to the valley in the spring of 1763.
What Indians lived here at that time?
Who was responsible for the death of Chief Teedyuscung?
When was the first massacre in the **Wyoming Valley**?

Tell what you know about this terrible massacre.

What steps did the Governor of Pennsylvania take to drive out the Indians?

Why did the King of England refuse to allow further settlements in the Wyoming Valley?

IV

PROPRIETARIES BEGIN SETTLEMENT OF WYOMING VALLEY

"Now, children, yesterday I told you of the sad ending of the first white settlement in the Wyoming Valley in October, 1763. Well, it was during this same year, 1763, that the French and Indian War was declared at an end by the Treaty of Paris. By this treaty, England came into possession of all the territory claimed by the French east of the Mississippi River," Grandmother continued.

With the ending of hostilities between the French and English colonists, the Indian tribes who had allied themselves with the French again became friendly with the English. The colonists now thought the time favorable to establish boundaries between the Indian and English claims. With this end in view, a meeting was finally arranged with the Indians at Fort Stanwix, N. Y., in 1768, at which a general treaty was made.[1] At this meeting several of the Indian chiefs signed a deed transferring to the Proprietaries of Pennsylvania all the land included in the province of Pennsylvania, and not already sold to them. By this transaction the Proprietaries secured the Indian title to all the lands included in the present State of Pennsylvania. The Wyoming Valley, that had been previously sold to the Susquehanna Company by the Six Nations, was included in this sale.

The Proprietaries now began to make plans for the settlement of Wyoming in order to establish their claim. They did not follow the plan adopted by the Susquehanna Company seven years before. You will

---

[1] November 5, 1768.

remember the Susquehanna Company sent about two hundred men into the valley, each man having the right to select a claim and develop it. After a residence of five years in the valley, the Connecticut settler would own the claim he had developed.

The Proprietaries leased the valley to three men (Amos Ogden, Charles Stuart, and John Jennings) for a period of seven years. In this lease the lessees agreed to establish a house to be used as a trading station for the Indians. They further agreed to provide protection for those who, with their possessions, might settle in the valley under their jurisdiction.

Mr. Chapman tells us that Charles Stuart, who was a surveyor, laid out the valley in two manors. The one on the east side of the river was known as the "Manor of Stoke." The one on the west side was known as the "Manor of Sunbury." Tillsbury Knob, the high peak of the mountain back of West Nanticoke, originally part of the "Manor of Sunbury," is the only land in the State still owned by the heirs of William Penn.

The Pennsylvania lessees arrived in the valley in January, 1769, and they at once took possession of the remains of the settlement at the mouth of Mill Creek, from which the Delawares had so cruelly driven the Connecticut settlers in 1763.

SUSQUEHANNA COMPANY PLANS TO AGAIN TAKE UP THE SETTLEMENT OF THE WYOMING VALLEY. CONNECTICUT SETTLERS ARRIVE IN VALLEY. FIND THEIR OLD SETTLEMENT AT MILL CREEK IN POSSESSION OF THE PROPRIETARIES. BEGINNING OF PENNAMITE-YANKEE WARS.

A short time after the treaty was made with the Indians at Fort Stanwix in 1768, the members of the

SETTLEMENT OF WYOMING VALLEY 43

Susquehanna Company began to consider the advisability of again establishing their claim in the Wyoming Valley. For this purpose a meeting was held in Hartford, Connecticut, on December 28th, of that year, and forty men, members of the company, were empowered to take possession of the Susquehanna Purchase by the following February 1st, with the understanding that two hundred additional persons would join them not later than May 1st.

At this meeting plans were made for the development of the valley. The committee in charge was instructed to lay out five townships, three on one side of the river and two on the opposite side. Each township was to be five miles square, and the first forty settlers were to be given a choice of townships.

Plans were also made for the establishment of religion and schools in the new settlement.

Five men were named by the officers of the company to take charge of all business for the first forty settlers.

In those days, as you know, they didn't have the wonderful highways we have today. In fact, they did not even have dirt roads. The settlers who had traveled to the Wyoming Valley from Connecticut up to this time had followed the Indian trails when possible, and then struggled on through the wilderness until they had reached their destination. With plans for a new settlement before them, the members of the company began to consider the need of a road for the transportation of the possessions of the new colony. They, therefore, instructed the committee to lay out and get ready "a convenient road" from Connecticut to their claim on the Susquehanna River.

And so, on February 8, 1769, the forty persons appointed by the Susquehanna Company to again take up the settlement of the Susquehanna Purchase arrived in the valley and proceeded to the site of their old settlement at the mouth of Mill Creek.

Of course, they knew that their former homes had been burned by the Indians in 1763, and you can imagine their surprise when, on arriving at their claim, they were confronted by a fortified blockhouse built on the plot of ground they had cleared and cultivated about six years before. At first they could not understand who had erected this building, but soon learned that it belonged to the Proprietaries, and was occupied by some of the Pennsylvania claimants. Later they were told that the Proprietaries of Pennsylvania had leased the valley to some of the men in possession, and these men, fearing trouble with the Connecticut colonists, had fortified themselves against invasion.

Determined to get possession of their former settlement, the Yankees, as the Connecticut settlers were called, decided the best plan would be to surround the blockhouse, and thus prevent the occupants from communicating with their friends. They at once began to cut down trees, which were speedily converted into huts that surrounded the blockhouse.

A few days before the arrival of the Yankees in the valley the Pennamites, or Pennsylvanians, had learned of their approach, and had sent a messenger to the Governor to ask for food and reinforcements.

After waiting for some time, and despairing of receiving any help from the Governor, the Pennamites hit upon a plan to outwit the Yankees. A note was sent to the Yankee headquarters inviting some of their leaders to the blockhouse to talk over the question of their claims so that matters could be settled peaceably.

The invitation was gladly accepted by three of the Yankees, who were anxious for an amicable settlement, and they at once proceeded to the place of meeting.

BURNING OF WYOMING

SETTLEMENT OF WYOMING VALLEY 45

Now, one of the Pennsylvania lessees, John Jennings, was sheriff of Northampton County, and as soon as the Yankees entered the blockhouse he arrested them. He then took them to Easton, where he placed them in prison. They did not remain prisoners long, however, as bail was secured for them almost immediately by some of their friends who had accompanied them. Upon their release they returned to Wyoming.

And now began a civil war between the Proprietaries of Pennsylvania and the Connecticut settlers for the possession of the Wyoming Valley, a war that caused bloodshed, suffering, and privation and lasted for many years, and was known as the Pennamite-Yankee War.

THE PENNAMITE-YANKEE WAR. YANKEES ERECT FORT DURKEE. EXPEDITION AGAINST FORT DURKEE. YANKEES SEEK A PEACEFUL SETTLEMENT OF CLAIMS. SECOND EXPEDITION AGAINST FORT DURKEE. THIRD EXPEDITION. PENNAMITES GET POSSESSION. YANKEES DRIVEN OUT OF VALLEY. (1769)

Upon their return to the valley the Yankees fortified a house for their protection against the Pennamites. In March, having learned of the approach of Sheriff Jennings at the head of a body of Pennsylvanians, the Yankees at once secured themselves in their stronghold. It proved inadequate, however, as the Pennamites on arriving succeeded in forcing an entrance, and seized nearly all the inmates. The whole party of Yankees were then taken to Easton where they were imprisoned. They were later released on bail.

During the following month, April, 1769, the two hundred additional settlers sent by the Susquehanna Company arrived in the valley. As soon as they learned of the attacks of the Pennamites they began the erection of a fort for the protection of the little colony. The site selected by them was on the river bank in the present city of Wilkes-Barre, and the place where it stood is now marked by a monument. This fortification was named Fort Durkee in honor of Captain Durkee, one of their number, and consisted of a blockhouse built of logs surrounded by a rampart and intrenchment. Near the fort about twenty loghouses were built by the Yankees for the use of the colony. Each house was provided with loopholes so that if the settlers were attacked suddenly and could not reach the fort they could protect themselves by firing on the enemy without being exposed. In addition to the fortification erected by the settlers, nature had provided two barriers that helped to insure protection to the Yankees, the Susquehanna River on one side and a marsh and brook (from what is now the lower part of the square down to Riverside Drive) on the other. With so many barriers the Yankees felt that the fort would afford them a secure refuge when needed.

Jennings and Ogden (two of the lessees of the Proprietaries), who had been away from the valley for a few weeks were doubtless very much surprised when they returned and saw what the Yankees had accomplished in so short a time. They at once decided to dispossess them and approached the fort with a body of Pennsylvanians. They arrived before the Yankee stronghold in May, but finding the fortification too strong abandoned their plan and returned to Easton.

The Yankees felt safe in their well-fortified position, and now turned their attention to the cultivation of the land and other improvements. The site of our county seat was selected by Captain Durkee, who named it Wilkes-Barre in honor of John Wilkes and Colonel

SETTLEMENT OF WYOMING VALLEY 47

Isaac Barre, who were ardent supporters of the cause of liberty.

Hoping to avoid further trouble with the Pennamites the Yankees sent two of their number to Philadelphia to try and settle the dispute. Their proposition was not given any consideration. The Proprietaries were determined to get possession of the territory, and were at that time making plans for an attack.

A short time later Colonel Francis was sent by the Proprietaries at the head of an armed force to take possession of Fort Durkee. This expedition arrived in the valley June 22, 1769. Colonel Francis' demand for surrender was ignored by the Yankees, and after ascertaining the strength of the fort he withdrew his force without making an attack.

The failure of Colonel Francis' expedition only made the Proprietaries more determined to get possession of the Wyoming Valley. Their next plan was to send Sheriff Jennings, of Northampton County, at the head of a large force to seize Fort Durkee. By September Jennings had succeeded in getting together a sufficiently large number to make an attack, and at once took up his march to Wyoming. He carried with him firearms, ammunition and an iron four-pounder together with provisions.

Having learned of Jennings' approach, Captain Ogden, who was located in the valley, at the head of about forty armed men, made a surprise attack on the Yankees and took several prisoners. Colonel Durkee, one of the Yankee leaders, who was among the number seized by Ogden, was taken to Philadelphia and imprisoned there.

Jennings, in command of a force of about two hundred men, arrived in the valley two days later. Upon his arrival he assembled his men before the fort, but failed to force a surrender. The following day they again took up their position, and began the erection of a battery on which to mount the four-pounder to besiege the fort. The garrison were not prepared to withstand a siege of this kind and decided to surrender.

The terms of capitulation provided that seventeen men were to remain in possession of the settlers' property in order to hold their claim, and to harvest and care for the grain they had sowed. They were to remain in the valley until the king's decision regarding the right to the disputed territory should be made known. The Yankees now vacated the settlement with the exception of the men left to care for their claim.

Ogden did not keep faith with the Yankees long, and with his men soon began to plunder the settlement. Livestock and other movable property were seized and disposed of at the market on the Delaware. They left nothing for the maintenance of the men who were in charge of the Connecticut claim.

The prospect of starvation in the Wyoming Valley during the long winter months did not appeal to the Yankees, and, abandoning their claim, they returned to Connecticut leaving the Proprietaries in possession of the valley.

After the departure of the Yankees the Pennsylvania leaders also left the valley. Ten men remained as a garrison to hold possession of the Proprietaries' interests.

And so the close of the year 1769 found the Pennamites in possession of the Wyoming Valley.

FIFTH DAY

Grandmother continued her practice of asking questions on the story of the previous day. The following are the questions for the fifth day of the story:

When did the French and Indian War end?

HON. JOHN WILKES

SETTLEMENT OF WYOMING VALLEY 49

Why did the English consider this a good time to establish boundaries?

Tell what you know about the meeting held in Fort Stanwix in 1768.

What plan did the Pennsylvania claimants follow to begin the settlement of the Wyoming Valley?

How did they lay out the valley?

What were the two manors called?

When did the lessees and their party arrive in the valley?

Where did they establish their first settlement?

What was done at the meeting of the Susquehanna Company held in Hartford in 1768?

When did the Connecticut settlers arrive in the valley?

How did they feel when they found their old settlement in possession of the Pennamites?

What did they proceed to do?

Why did the Pennamites send a messenger to the governor for help when they heard the Connecticut settlers were on their way to the valley?

When the Pennamites failed to get help what plan did they put into effect to outwit the Yankees?

Did the Yankees remain long in prison?

When did the Pennamite-Yankee War begin?

What did the Yankees do upon their return to the valley?

Was the attack made by Sheriff Jennings and his party in March successful?

Did the Yankees remain in jail long?

How many Yankees arrived in Wyoming in April, 1769?

What fortification did they erect?

Describe it.

When did Jennings and Ogden attempt to take this fort?

Were they successful?

Did the Yankees try to secure a peaceful settlement of the dispute?

Why did the Proprietaries send Colonel Francis to Wyoming?

Did he succeed in taking the fort?

When was the next expedition put under way by the Proprietaries?

Who was in charge of this expedition?

Was the force well equipped?

What did Captain Ogden do?

What Yankee leader was among the prisoners taken?

Tell about the surrender of Fort Durkee.

How many men were left in possession?

Did the Pennamites live up to their agreement?

Why did the Yankees left in charge of the settlement return to Connecticut?

What party had possession of the Wyoming Valley at the close of 1769?

V

(1770) CAPTURE OF FORT DURKEE BY YANKEES

After the return of the Yankee Colonists to Connecticut the members of the Susquehanna Company again got busy. A meeting was held at Windham, Conn., January 10, 1770, at which the Standing Committee were directed "to proceed in what they esteemed best for the interest of the Company to keep and maintain their purchase on the Susquehanna River."

Lazarus Stewart, a Yankee leader, coming up from Lancaster County at the head of a body of settlers from that place, together with a number of Connecticut Yankees, who had the authority of the Susquehanna Company back of them, reached the Valley in February, 1770. The Pennamites, who did not expect the Yankee colonists to return at such an early date, had only a few men defending Fort Durkee for the winter months and the Yankees at once took possession of that stronghold.

Their next move was to get possession of the four-pounder that had played such a prominent part in forcing them to surrender Fort Durkee the year previous. They proceeded to Ogden's Fort at Mill Creek, where they knew the cannon was stored and, after securing possession of it, returned in triumph to Fort Durkee.

Ogden, who had been away from the Valley, upon hearing of the Yankees' success in securing possession of Fort Durkee and the four-pounder hurriedly returned to Wyoming and with his party took possession of the blockhouse which he fortified against the Yankees.

A short time after the Pennamites returned to the valley a small party made up of about ten Yankees arrived in Wyoming to re-enforce the garrison at Fort Durkee. Unaware of the presence of the Pennamites in the Valley they approached the Fort at Mill Creek, which they believed to be garrisoned by the Yankees. They were immediately taken prisoners by Ogden and his men, and so closely were they confined, that it was not until the surrender of the fort about a month later that their friends at Fort Durkee learned of their presence in the Valley.

The Yankees now decided that the best course to pursue would be to make Ogden prisoner, and so, on March 28, 1770, about fifty Yankees from Fort Durkee approached Ogden's blockhouse at Mill Creek with the intention of making him prisoner. Now among the party that accompanied Ogden back to Wyoming was a deputy sheriff, who was in the house at the time, and with aid of the Proprietaries' force, he attempted to turn the tables on the Yankees and make them prisoners. A fight took place in which several of the Yankees were wounded and one man, William Stager, killed. This was the first blood spilled in the Pennamite-Yankee War, and neither party would assume the responsibility for having fired the first shot.

The Yankees now returned to Fort Durkee to plan further movements to force Ogden and his party to vacate the blockhouse.

After carefully considering the situation, they moved to the west side of the river and began the erection of a blockhouse opposite Ogden's place of refuge. This building was strongly fortified, and the four-pounder which they had taken from Ogden's house was

COL. ISAAC BARRÉ

CAPTURE OF FORT DURKEE 53

mounted there. On April 15th they began an attack on Ogden's fortification with the four-pounder. This lasted for several days, but was not successful. Another form of attack was now planned.

They again returned to the east side of the river and, on April 23, 1770, approached Ogden's house. After forming in three divisions, each party began to erect a breastwork. About noon of the same day fire was opened from all three on the blockhouse. Ogden's party returned the fire and this continued at intervals for five days.

On the third day of the siege the Yankees set fire to one of Ogden's houses which was burned to the ground together with a large quantity of supplies and food.

In the meantime, Captain Durkee, who had been released from prison in Philadelphia, had returned to the Valley. On April 28th he requested Captain Ogden to meet him in conference.

As a result of this meeting, the Pennamites vacated the blockhouse, with the exception of six men who remained to care for Ogden's property.

After the departure of the Pennamites from the Valley, the Yankees, forgetting their agreement, took possession of Ogden's property and burned the blockhouse.

THE GOVERNOR'S PROCLAMATION, JUNE, 1770

Now, right after the attack of the Yankees on the blockhouse, March 28, 1770, when William Stager was killed, Ogden wrote the Governor for reinforcements to drive the Yankees out of the Valley. No help being available in Pennsylvania, the Governor in turn appealed to the British commander, General Gage, for help. He did not get any co-operation from that quarter, as General Gage did not think it right for the king's troops to take up the fight, as it appeared to be a dispute over property.

The Governor, disappointed in his efforts to secure reinforcements, now tried another plan to force the Yankees to leave the Wyoming Valley. On June 28, 1770, he issued a proclamation ordering all intruders to vacate the Wyoming Valley, and forbidding the settlement of any part of the Valley without the consent of the Proprietaries.

OGDEN MARCHES TO WYOMING AT THE HEAD OF A FORCE OF ONE HUNDRED FORTY MEN. MAKES A SURPRISE ATTACK ON FORT DURKEE AND TAKES MANY PRISONERS

The Governor, having failed to secure military aid, now decided to fall back on the Proprietaries' resources. By September the services of one hundred forty men had been secured. These were placed under Captain Ogden's command, and then the march to Wyoming began.

Captain Ogden knew that the main path into the Valley, which had been used for previous invasions, would be carefully watched by the Yankees, and so he marched by way of Fort Allen on the Lehigh River, and from there proceeded on the Warriors' Path to Wyoming. Chapman tells us that this is the route he followed, and that on September 21st he encamped with his men in Solomon's Gap.

His previous knowledge of the strength of the fort now proved of great value to him. He decided that the only way to take this Yankee stronghold would be to come upon the garrison unexpectedly when they were not prepared for an attack. After spending the night in the Gap, he moved his force to a point where they could command a view of the Valley without being seen by the Yankees.

CAPTURE OF FORT DURKEE

As in 1763, the unsuspecting settlers went to work in the fields without a thought of the danger lurking in the near-by mountains. Ogden, from his post, watched them separate, every man going to his own claim, and he decided to attack them while they were unprotected at their labors.

Dividing his force into several parties, attacks were made from all sides about the same time. Many of the settlers were seized and sent to Easton jail. A large number, however, succeeded in reaching the fort which they prepared to defend. With the approach of night, Ogden withdrew his men to the shelter of Solomon's Gap.

The surprise attack by Captain Ogden and his men was a great blow to the Yankees. Many of their men had been made prisoners, and the remaining inmates of Fort Durkee were now thoroughly alarmed. A consultation was held, and it was decided to send messengers to the settlement of Coshutunk on the Delaware for help. Fearing the Pennamites would anticipate such a move and place guards on the direct road to the Delaware, the Yankees decided to take a less frequented path. It was much longer, but to the Yankees seemed more secure. This route, unfortunately, led through Solomon's Gap where the Pennamites were encamped. Unaware of their presence, the messengers approached the Gap and were immediately seized and made prisoners by the Pennamites.

Ogden now decided to make an attack on the fort at once under cover of darkness, and at a time when the Yankees were not prepared to offer resistance. This move proved a good one for the Pennamites. The Yankees were forced to surrender, and many of the garrison were imprisoned at Easton. Captain Butler and a few others were placed in prison in Philadelphia. (September 23, 1770.)

56 PIONEER DAYS IN WYOMING VALLEY

The victors now helped themselves to all movable property and then departed for their homes. About eighteen of their number were left behind to hold possession of the fort.

YANKEES RETURN TO VALLEY AND SEIZE FORT DURKEE. CAPTAIN LAZARUS STEWART IN CHARGE OF GARRISON. CLOSE OF YEAR 1770

With the departure of the Connecticut settlers from the Valley, the Pennamites felt they had nothing further to worry about. The Yankees, however, did not share their opinion, for about three o'clock on the morning of December 18, 1770, a surprise attack was made on the fort by a small party of Yankees.

Six of the garrison escaped to the woods, but the other twelve were taken prisoners, and with women and children driven from the Valley.

Captain Lazarus Stewart, in command of the Yankees, now took possession of the fort. The close of the year 1770 finds the Connecticut settlers in possession of the Wyoming Valley.

SIXTH DAY

Grandmother was at her post on time and found her class waiting to greet her. The number had been steadily growing, and she welcomed a much larger audience than that of the first day. As usual, she was armed with her list of questions. Can you answer all of them?

> Were the members of the Susquehanna Company satisfied to give up their claim to the Susquehanna Purchase?
> When did the Yankees again return to Wyoming?

CAPTURE OF FORT DURKEE 57

Who was their leader? On arriving in the Valley, what did they do?

What effect did this move have on the Pennamites?

How did the Yankees proceed to take Ogden prisoner?

Were they succsesful?

Who was the first man killed in the Pennamite-Yankee War?

Which party fired the first shot?

What was the next move by the Yankees?

When did the Pennamites surrender?

What did the Yankees do after the Pennamites left the Valley?

Tell me about the Governor's Proclamation in June, 1770, and the circumstances that led up to it.

When did Captain Ogden again return to the Valley?

What route did he follow?

Where did his troops camp at night?

Tell about his surprise attack on the Yankees.

To whom did the Yankees appeal for help?

Did the messengers reach their destination?

How did Captain Ogden get possession of Fort Durkee?

Did he remain long in the Valley?

When did the Yankees return to their settlement?

What colony held possession of the Wyoming Valley at the close of 1770?

VI

THE EVENTS OF 1771

"Well, children," continued Grandmother, "I am glad to find you all so interested in the history of the Valley, and I am sorry some of you have not been here for all the story. Now we will take up the history where we left off yesterday—today you will hear the events of 1771."

At the time of the burning of Captain Ogden's house in the spring of 1770, a warrant was issued by the Supreme Court of Pennsylvania, authorizing the arrest of Lazarus Stewart for the crime of arson.

Upon learning that Captain Stewart was in charge of the garrison at Fort Durkee, the Proprietaries at once sent Peter Hacklein, sheriff of Northampton County, armed with a warrant to arrest him. Accompanied by Amos Ogden at the head of a large force, he set out for the Wyoming Valley, arriving here January 18, 1771. Stewart, who was a member of the Connecticut colony, refused to recognize the authority of the Proprietaries' officer, and the sheriff was unable to serve the warrant.

Ogden and his men, on arriving in the Valley, began to build a blockhouse to take the place of the one burned by the Yankees. Hacklein and his party now joined the Pennamites and helped them build the house and erect fortifications to insure safety. The work on the fort was finished Sunday night, January 19th, and the morning of Monday, January 20th, the trouble between the Pennamites and Yankees began again.

Amos Ogden and the sheriff, accompanied by their

THE EVENTS OF 1771

men, approached the fort and demanded admittance, which was promptly refused. They at once opened fire and the volley was returned by the garrison. Nathan Ogden, a brother of Amos, was killed and three men were wounded.

The Pennamites, after securing the bodies of their fallen comrade and the wounded men, returned to their quarters. A conference was held and no further action was taken during the day.

Under cover of darkness, Stewart, with about forty of his men, fled from the fort, leaving twelve men in charge. The following day these men surrendered the fort to the Pennamites.

The Governor was wrathful over the death of Nathan Ogden, and, upon recommendation of the General Assembly, offered a reward of three hundred pounds for the capture of Lazarus Stewart.

The sheriff now turned the fort over to Amos Ogden and marched to Easton with his prisoners. Several of the Pennamites, who had been driven out of the Valley by the Yankees, again took up their residence here under Ogden's protection, and all was peaceful in the Valley until July, 1771.

YANKEES ATTACK WYOMING FORT. CUT PENNAMITES OFF FROM RELIEF. CAPTAIN OGDEN ESCAPES, REACHES PHILADELPHIA, AND INFORMS COUNCIL OF SERIOUS CONDITION AT WYOMING. PLANS MADE BY PENNAMITES TO RELIEVE THEIR GARRISON AT THAT PLACE. SIEGE OF FORT WYOMING. FORT SURRENDERS. YANKEES IN POSSESSION OF THE VALLEY. END OF THE FIRST PENNAMITE-YANKEE WAR, AUGUST, 1771

After having endured nearly three years of almost continuous strife, the beautiful Wyoming Valley must have welcomed the interval of peace. But this calm was rudely broken on July 6, 1771, when the Connecticut settlers, under the command of Captain Zebulon Butler and Captain Lazarus Stewart, entered the Valley, determined to wrest the possession of their claim from the Pennamites. Captain Ogden's party, the only inhabitants of the Valley, was made up of about eighty-two persons. On the approach of the enemy they fled to the protection of a new fort which Ogden had built on the bank of the river between Fort Durkee and Mill Creek, and which he had named Wyoming Fort.

For the first three days the Yankees did not make an attack. They were no doubt carefully considering the best way to force the Pennamites to surrender. On the night of the third day, under cover of darkness, the Yankees began to build entrenchments on the east side of the river which would command the fort. After completing these, they began the erection of a similar entrenchment on the west side to prevent escape from the fort by way of the river. A few days later Yankee reinforcements arrived in the Valley, and the inmates of Wyoming Fort were cut off from all communication with their friends. The Yankees felt they had left no loophole for escape.

Although the fort was surrounded on all sides, Captain Ogden would not give up. He was determined to get help for the little band in his charge, and he knew the only way to get it was to go after it. And that reminds me of another little verse that I heard many years ago.

> All things come to him who waits,
> But here's a rule that's slicker;
> The man who goes for what he wants,
> Will get it all the quicker.

BLOCKHOUSE.

THE EVENTS OF 1771

So, under cover of darkness on the night of July 12th, tying some of his clothes in a bundle on the top of which he placed his hat, he attached them to his body with a long piece of line, and, dropping into the river, floated downstream, his clothes following him several feet in the rear. Ogden kept his body well under water, but his clothes were observed by the Yankee sentinels, who commenced firing at them. The shots did not affect the uniform motion of the dark object, and the firing ceased. After passing the danger zone, Captain Ogden climbed up the bank, dressed, and started on his long journey to Philadelphia, where he arrived three days later. He was unharmed, but his clothes had been penetrated by several shots.

Captain Ogden, by this act, proved himself an honorable and brave man. You will remember that he was one of the three men to whom the Valley was leased by the Proprietaries. You will also remember that the lessees agreed to protect the people settling under them. Captain Ogden, in this instance, tried to protect the people in his care at the risk of his own life.

On his arrival in Philadelphia he immediately informed the council of the serious situation at Wyoming, and steps were at once taken to relieve the garrison at that place.

Plans were made to hire one hundred men to be placed under Colonel Asher Clayton's command in two divisions, one in charge of Captain Joseph Morris and the other in charge of Captain John Dick. An appropriation of three hundred pounds was made to cover expenses as these men would need equipment and provisions.

Much difficulty was experienced in raising the required number. Captain Dick, in charge of a small company of about thirty-six men and carrying provisions for about three times that number, arrived in the Wyoming Valley at daybreak Tuesday, July 30th. The Connecticut settlers, who had learned of his approach, were awaiting his arrival. They attacked him from ambush, and only twenty-two of his company reached the fort. The remainder, with horses and provisions, were taken by the Yankees.

The Yankees now opened fire on Fort Wyoming from the intrenchments, and this continued for eleven days. On the 11th of August, 1771, Captain Butler sent a flag and demanded the surrender of the fort, which was refused. The siege was resumed and continued for three days longer, when the fort surrendered, August 14, 1771. During this long siege, several men of the Pennsylvania party were wounded, and one man, William Ridyard, killed.

Now, after Captain Dick's arrival in the Valley, he succeeded in getting a messenger past the Yankee lines with a message to the council at Philadelphia informing them of his unfortunate experience.

Greatly alarmed at the situation, the council at once planned to raise an additional hundred men to reinforce the number already in the Valley. They also appropriated another three hundred pounds to defray the expenses of this company.

Sixty of this number, under the command of Captain Ledlie, were on their way to the Wyoming Valley to relieve the Pennamites, and were just about ten miles from the settlement, when the fort surrendered. Upon learning that the Yankees had secured possession of the Valley, Captain Ledlie stationed his men in the mountains leading to Wyoming, and placed guards along the roads to prevent the arrival of reinforcements from the Connecticut colony.

The Proprietaries now withdrew their troops and

THE EVENTS OF 1771

left the Connecticut settlers in possession of the coveted territory.

Thus ended the first Pennamite-Yankee War which began in 1769 and covered a period of almost three years. These years of suffering and privation were, no doubt, long remembered with aching hearts and many regrets by both Yankees and Pennamites.

WYOMING ENJOYS DAYS OF PEACE. SUSQUEHANNA COMPANY APPOINTS AGENT TO CONFER WITH GOVERNOR PENN. MILL CREEK FORT REPAIRED AND OCCUPIED. MEETINGS HELD. SETTLERS ORDERED TO ARM AND EQUIP THEMSELVES FOR THE PROTECTION OF THE COLONY. GUARDS ON DUTY

With the withdrawal of the Pennamite troops, peace at last settled on the Wyoming Valley.

The Yankees, while still determined to prosecute their claim to the Susquehanna Purchase, wanted to avoid future trouble with the Pennamites. And so, at a meeting of the Susquehanna Company, held at Norwich, Conn., April 1, 1772, Captain Joseph Trumbull was appointed agent for the company. He was instructed to call upon Governor Penn and confer with him regarding the best plan to adjust the claims of the Susquehanna Company and the Proprietaries of Pennsylvania.

The Yankees, while busily engaged in the cultivation of the soil and other improvements, were constantly on the alert for an attack from the Indians on the north or the Proprietaries on the south. The settlement was easily accessible from either end of the Valley. The settlers now moved to the forts for protection, and every man was armed at his work.

The Ogden fortification at the mouth of Mill Creek was repaired and fortified. The settlers from in and around Wilkes-Barre at once took advantage of the shelter of this now friendly fort, bringing their possessions with them.

Standing on the bank of the Susquehanna River, the fort was protected by natural barriers on two sides, the river on one side and Mill Creek on the other. This historic spot, the site of the first settlement in the Wyoming Valley, is near the present General Hospital on North River Street, Wilkes-Barre.

The early settlers in the Valley did not have the comforts and conveniences we have today. To give you an idea of the many privations they suffered, I will tell you what I have learned from the description of the interior of Fort Ogden given by Mr. Miner in his history.

The walls of the fort must have enclosed a very large plot, as Mr. Miner tells us that huts one story in height were built in the enclosure against the walls. Several of them were large enough to be divided into a number of small rooms. In addition to these homes for the settlers, there was also a store from which they could secure supplies, and a boarding house.

The furniture, which was of rude construction, had all been made in the Valley, and represented many hours of hard labor by the colonists.

Their only grist mill was a large tree stump, hollowed about ten inches by burning. In this hollow, corn, wheat, or rye was placed, and then pounded with a pestle. The coarse grain thus obtained was used for bread. Deer were abundant and easily secured, and the Susquehanna furnished a plentiful supply of shad, but seasoning, so necessary to make the food palatable, was hard to get. If any of the settlers wanted flour, they would have to travel by bridle path many miles to Coshutunk (now Stroudsburg) on the Delaware where a grist mill was located.

WYOMING FORT

THE EVENTS OF 1771

Many meetings were held, and each of these meetings was known as a "Meeting of the Proprietors." The presiding officer was called a "moderator" and served only for one meeting, a new man being elected every time a meeting was held.

In November, 1772, a "Meeting of the Proprietors" was held, and every owner of a settling right was ordered to "provide himself with a good firelock and ammunition according to the laws of Connecticut." (A "settling right" was the tract of land that had been taken up by one of the settlers and was being developed by him.) The land holders were given until the first Monday in December, 1772, to properly equip themselves, and were further instructed to then appear complete in arms at the fort in Wilkes-Barre at twelve o'clock "on said day for drilling as ye law directs." The people of every town in the Valley were empowered to elect a muster officer and inspector who would have the privilege of selecting two sergeants and a clerk. It was also ordered that a meeting of the settlers, armed and equipped, should be held every fourteen days. In case of an attack, the inhabitants were instructed to unite for the defense of the settlement without further orders. In October, 1772, it was decreed that any man who failed to do his duty for the protection of the Valley would lose his settling right.

Many settlers had immigrated to the Valley during 1772, and so great were the needs of the colony that, by February, 1773, the food supply was almost exhausted, and it was found necessary to send to the Delaware for provisions. With the approach of spring and the opening of the fishing season, food was again plentiful.

Guards were kept on duty day and night during the years 1772 and 1773. During this period of uneasiness the settlers were busy completing plans for the protection of their colony. A stockade was erected at Plymouth, Hanover was fortified with a blockhouse, and Forty Fort was repaired. The dwellings were all loopholed, and every settler's home was his private fort, well provided with means of defense.

SEVENTH DAY

On the sixth day, Grandmother had led the children through a recital of the stirring events of 1771 up to the close of the first Pennamite-Yankee War, the days of peace that followed, and the activities of the settlers. The following are the questions Grandmother required her audience to answer on the seventh day. Won't you try and answer all of them, too?

Why was Peter Hacklein sent to the Valley to arrest Lazarus Stewart?

Did he succeed in serving the warrant?

What did Ogden and his men do on reaching the Valley?

When was the blockhouse completed?

What did the Pennamites do the following day?

Tell about the death of Nathan Ogden.

When did Fort Durkee surrender?

What reward was offered for the capture of Lazarus Stewart?

Who now took charge of Fort Durkee?

How long did the interval of peace last?

When did trouble again begin in the Valley?

Who commanded the Connecticut settlers?

Where did the Pennamites fortify themselves?

How did the Yankees cut the Pennamites off from communication with their friends?

Tell the story of Captain Ogden's daring and bravery.

THE EVENTS OF 1771

What did the council at Philadelphia do upon learning of the situation at Wyoming?

Tell about the surrender of Fort Wyoming and the events leading up to it.

What captain was on the way to the Valley to relieve the Pennamites when the fort surrendered?

When did the first Pennamite-Yankee War end?

Who was appointed agent for the Susquehanna Company?

What was he instructed to do?

Where did the settlers from in and around Wilkes-Barre take up their residence?

Where was the first settlement in the Wyoming Valley located?

Tell all you know about the interior of Mill Creek Fort.

What were the meetings of the settlers called?

What was done at the meeting held in November, 1772?

What caused the scarcity of food during the winter of 1772-1773?

Did the settlers make any plans for the protection of the colony?

VII

IMPORTANT MEETING OF THE SUSQUEHANNA COMPANY AT HARTFORD

Now we must leave the Wyoming Valley and go back to Connecticut to learn what was done at a meeting held in Hartford, June 2, 1773.

At this meeting the members, after swearing allegiance to King George III., agreed to live soberly and peacefully.

They then planned to improve conditions in the settlement at Wyoming.

It was agreed to choose three able and judicious men in each town to take upon themselves the direction of the settlement of said town, suppress vice, and preserve peace. The inhabitants of every town under the jurisdiction of the Susquehanna Company were empowered to choose one trustworthy person to be their "peace officer," this man to have the same "power and authority as a constable."

It was also agreed that the directors in each town should meet on the first Monday of the month, or oftener if necessary, with their peace officers in order to properly adjust all matters needing their attention.

It was further agreed that the directors of the several towns should once every quarter meet together in order to discuss conditions existing in the different towns of the settlement.

The first Monday in December was appointed for the selection of directors, the peace officer, and other officers necessary.

MORTAR AND PESTLE

MEETING AT HARTFORD

In every town in the settlement the directors were required to keep a copy of the agreement to be signed by every male inhabitant attaining the age of twenty-one years. Any man refusing to sign the agreement was prohibited from settling in the Wyoming Valley.

The following directors were appointed to serve until the first Monday in December, 1773:

Major John Durkee, Captain Zebulon Butler, Obadiah Gore, Jr.—For the town of Wilkes-Barre.

Phineas Nash, Captain David Marvin, Joseph Gaylord—For the town of Plymouth.

Isaac Tripp, Esq., Timothy Keys, Gideon Baldwin—For the town of New Providence (now Scranton).

Captain Obadiah Gore, Nathan Denison, Parshall Terry—For the town of Kingston.

Captain Lazarus Stewart, William Stewart, John Franklin—For the town of Hanover.

Caleb Bates, James Brown, Lemuel Harding—For the town of Pittstown.

Major Durkee, Captain Zebulon Butler, Obadiah Gore, Jr., and Nathan Denison were appointed a committee for the laying out of townships.

And while these plans were being made at Hartford for the benefit of the colony, the settlers in the Valley were not idle. They made and enforced laws, and also formed a militia, the members of which acted as a garrison in the forts for the protection of the colonists and their possessions, and took turns at guard duty. Every man in the settlement able to bear arms was a member of the militia, and its formation provided the patriot forces who defended the settlement at the Battle of Wyoming.

70 PIONEER DAYS IN WYOMING VALLEY

GENERAL ASSEMBLY AT NEW HAVEN. COMMITTEE CALLS ON GOVERNOR PENN. TOWN OF WESTMORELAND ESTABLISHED BY AN ACT OF THE CONNECTICUT LEGISLATURE

The next event of importance regarding the settlement in the Wyoming Valley occurred at New Haven, Connecticut, when a General Assembly of the Governor and Commissioners of the Connecticut Colony was held there in October, 1773.

This meeting was held on the second Thursday of the month, and the Assembly resolved that they would assert and in some proper way support their claim to the lands contained within the limits of the charter of the Connecticut Colony, westward of the Province of New York.

A committee was appointed to assist Governor Trumbull in pursuing the claims of the Connecticut Colony to the Westward Lands, any three of whom were authorized to proceed to Philadelphia to treat with Governor Penn and the agents of the Proprietaries of Pennsylvania regarding a peaceable adjustment of the boundaries between the Connecticut Colony and the Province of Pennsylvania. And so three of the committee journeyed to Philadelphia to try and settle the dispute without further trouble.

Governor Penn refused to consider their appeal. He stated that when the Pennsylvania grant was made, neither the King nor William Penn, himself, understood that this grant "intrenched upon or approached near any of the New England grants."

He told them that the first intimation he had of the existence of such a condition was when the claim was made on the part of Connecticut. He further stated that he could not join them "in an application to the Crown for an appointment of commissioners to settle lines or boundaries, because that would be admitting what he totally denied, namely, that the lines of Pennsylvania and Connecticut intrenched upon or interfered with each other." He thought it would be wise to petition his Majesty for a decision as he was anxious for a speedy settlement. He advised the Susquehanna Company to withdraw their people from the settlements within the boundaries of Pennsylvania to which they had no legal right.

The members of the Susquehanna Company did not take the advice of the Governor of Pennsylvania, for they felt their claim was legal and right because of earlier grant and earlier purchase from the Indians than that of the Pennsylvania Government. Their people still retained possession of their claim in the Wyoming Valley, and in January, 1774, the Connecticut Legislature by an act established the town of Westmoreland, as a part of Litchfield County. Wyoming was a part of the territory included within the limits of this town.

The Yankee settlers were very much encouraged, as they felt they now had some authority back of them, and that their mother colony, Connecticut, would help them in time of need. This spurred them on to greater activity. Soon a prosperous settlement was established, land was cultivated, roads built, laws made and enforced, schools erected to care for the education of the young, and provision was made for the establishment of religion in the colony, and for the support of the ministry.

During the previous year, 1773, a grist mill had been built on Mill Creek by Nathan Chapman, and a few months later a sawmill was erected on the same waters.

Residents were carried from the east to the west side of the Susquehanna by means of two ferries, one located at Mill Creek and one at Northampton

Street. (A ferry was a raft made large enough to drive a horse and wagon on, and was pushed or pulled across the river by hand. A rope stretched across the river, to which the ferry was attached, held it in position so that it would not float down the stream.)

The law governing the sale of intoxicants was very severe. Any settler convicted of selling liquor to an Indian would have to forfeit his possessions and leave the Valley.

To prevent trouble with overlapping claims, a land office was established in the colony.

And so that year, 1775, opens with a prosperous settlement, whose every inhabitant is working for the good of the community.

(1775) REVOLUTIONARY WAR BREAKS OUT. MEETING HELD IN TOWN OF WESTMORELAND. SETTLERS RESOLVE TO JOIN IN THE COMMON CAUSE OF LIBERTY

The Yankees, while making every effort to build up and improve the settlement, were constantly on the alert for an attack. War had broken out between the Colonies and England. In the Wyoming Valley the northern boundaries of the settlement were exposed to attacks from the savage Indians, and the need of untiring vigilance can be appreciated. The trouble which had sprung up between England and the Colonies, however, dwarfed the local troubles in comparison, and every man was anxious to fight for the rights of the Colonies and liberty.

A meeting of the proprietors and settlers of the town of Westmoreland was legally warned and held in Westmoreland, August 1, 1775.

> Mr. John Jenkins was chosen Moderator for ye work of ye day. Voted that this town does now vote that they will strictly observe and follow ye

MEETING AT HARTFORD

rules and regulations of ye Honorable Continental Congress, now sitting at Philadelphia.

Resolved by this town, that they are willing to make any accommodations with ye Pennsylvania Party that shall conduce to ye best good of ye whole, not infringing on the property of any person, and come in common cause of liberty in ye defence of America, and that we will amicably give them ye offer of joining in ye proposal as soon as may be.

At a meeting held one week later, August 8, 1775, it was

Voted as this town has but of late been incorporated and invested with the privileges of the law, both civil and military, and now in a capacity of acting in conjunction with our neighboring towns within this and other colonies, in opposing ye late measures adopted by Parliament to enslave America. Also this town having taken into consideration the late plan adopted by Parliament of enforcing their several oppressive and unconstitutional acts, of depriving us of our property, and of binding us in all cases without exception whether we consent or not, is considered by us highly injurious to American or English freedom; therefore, do consent to and acquiesce in the late proceedings and advice of the Continental Congress, and do rejoice that those measures are adopted, and so universally received throughout the Continent; and in conformity to the Eleventh article of the Association, we do now appoint a Committee to attentively observe the conduct of all persons within this town touching the rules and regulations prescribed by the Honorable Continental Congress, and will unanimously join our brethren in America in the common cause of defending our liberty.

74 PIONEER DAYS IN WYOMING VALLEY

The proceedings of both these meetings showed the spirit of the Wyoming Valley pioneers, who were willing to forget their own troubles until the struggle undertaken by their fellow colonists was won.

PLUNKETT'S EXPEDITION TO SECURE POSSESSION OF THE WYOMING VALLEY ENDS IN DEFEAT. ATTEMPT DOES NOT DAMPEN SPIRITS OF THE CONNECTICUT SETTLERS

While the inhabitants of the Wyoming Valley were making plans to aid the American colonists in the fight for liberty, an expedition against the Connecticut Colony at Wyoming was being started by some of the Pennsylvania claimants. The object of this expedition was to secure possession of the Wyoming Valley and drive the Yankees out.

You will remember that in April, 1769, two hundred Yankees arrived in the Wyoming Valley to join the first forty. On this journey they were accompanied by another body of settlers, about three hundred in number, who were on their way to the west branch of the Susquehanna which was also a part of the Susquehanna Purchase.

These men built two settlements on the west branch in the vicinity of Muncy. One was known as Charleston Township and the other Judea Township.

For a period of six years the Proprietaries permitted these townships to grow and develop, but on September 28, 1775, a body of militia marched from Sunbury up the west branch and drove the Yankees out of their settlements. Several were made prisoners and taken to Sunbury, where they were placed in jail.

Now it was just at this time that boats from the Wyoming Valley were plundered near Sunbury. The settlers in the Wyoming Valley, fearing an attack

MEETING AT HARTFORD 75

from the Pennamites, appealed to Congress for protection.

On November 4th, Congress ordered that the Assemblies of the colonies of Pennsylvania and Connecticut take immediate steps to prevent further hostilities.

The Governor of Pennsylvania, ignoring the order of Congress, authorized Colonel William Plunkett, who was also a civil magistrate, to secure the services of a large body of men and conduct them to the Wyoming Valley to "restore peace and good order" in that settlement.

At the head of a force of about seven hundred men Plunkett began his march to Wyoming. Arms, powder, and provisions were conveyed up the river on a large boat. Sheriff William Cook accompanied the expedition.

When the news of this move reached Philadelphia, Congress at once recommended that the Yankees and Pennamites immediately cease all hostilities "until the dispute can be legally decided." All property taken was to be given back to the original owners. Both Yankees and Pennamites were to have the right to pass through the disputed territory either by land or water without being molested. All persons held prisoners were to be released.

Both parties were notified of the decision of Congress, but no action was taken by the Proprietaries to stay the invasion of Colonel Plunkett. Congress recommended the cessation of hostilities on December 20th, but Plunkett and his force continued their march along the Susquehanna. The river was full of floating ice, and the progress of the boat was slow.

Now, the Yankees were not sleeping at this time, but, as always, were on the alert for an attack, and, having learned of the movement of Plunkett's force, fortified themselves on a ridge of rocks on the west side of the river near Nanticoke Falls, which was along the line of march. (This ridge of rocks is known as "Rampart Rocks.") When the invaders reached this point, December 24, 1775, Plunkett decided to leave the boat, and after loading his men with supplies, started out on foot with no suspicion of the proximity of the settlers who were hiding near by.

On nearing the ridge, the Pennamites were met with a volley of musketry, and retreated in confusion. After some deliberation, Plunkett decided to enter the Valley by the east bank of the river, and began conveying his men to the other side. When about to land they were attacked from the east shore and one man was killed. The survivors tumbled into the boat and floated down the river. Plunkett, convinced that further efforts to get possession of Wyoming would no doubt end with a great loss to his troops, retreated from the Valley.

This attempt by the Pennamites to drive them out of the Valley did not dampen the spirits of the Connecticut settlers. They no doubt still remembered the stories of the oppression their fathers had suffered in England, and the desire for liberty obsessed them. Every man fit for military duty only awaited the call of Congress. All personal prejudices and party feelings were forgotten by these brave pioneers, and their greatest interest was in the common cause, the liberty of the colonies.

EIGHTH DAY

"Well, children," greeted Grandmother on the eighth day, "it makes me very happy to find you all so interested in my story of the Valley. I know it is a little hard to remember, but later, after I have told you all of it, we will have a review. So now get ready for your questions on yesterday's lesson."

MYERS' HOUSE.

MEETING AT HARTFORD 77

What was done by the Susquehanna Company at the meeting held in Hartford, June 2, 1773?

Were the settlers in the Wyoming Valley active at that time?

What was the purpose of the meeting held in October, 1773?

How did Governor Penn receive the Yankees' appeal?

What reply did he make?

Why did the Yankee settlers still retain their residence in the Valley?

When was the town of Westmoreland established?

What did the Wyoming Valley settlers do next?

When was the first grist mill built in the Valley?

How did the settlers travel with horses and wagons from the east to the west side of the river?

What can you tell me about the law governing the sale of intoxicants?

Why was a land office established?

Were the Wyoming Valley pioneers interested in the colonies' fight for liberty?

What was done at the meetings held August 1 and August 8, 1775?

Where were the Wyoming Valley boats plundered by the Pennamites?

Were the settlers in the Valley alarmed?

What action did Congress take?

Why was Colonel William Plunkett sent to the Wyoming Valley?

How many men were under his command? Tell all you know about this expedition. Was it successful?

Where is the ridge called "Rampart Rocks"?

Did this invasion by the Pennamites change the attitude of the Wyoming Valley settlers toward the other colonies?

VIII

PLANS MADE BY SETTLERS FOR PROTECTION OF WYOMING VALLEY

During the interval of peace, many of the Indians returned to the Valley. They were at first peaceful and friendly but later became hostile. As time went on their animosity toward the settlers increased. Realizing their inability to protect themselves from an attack by the Indians, the inhabitants of Wyoming appealed to their mother colony, Connecticut, for help. Their plea received no answer from that quarter, and, with aching hearts, they turned to Congress for aid.

The settlers waited for a while, until, finally discouraged with the inactivity of Congress in their case, they called a meeting and made plans for the protection of the settlements in the town of Westmoreland.

This meeting was called to order in Wilkes-Barre, District of Westmoreland, August 24, 1776. "Colonel Butler was chosen Moderator for ye work of ye day."

The meeting voted that

> It is the opinion of this meeting that it now becomes necessary for ye inhabitants of this town to erect suitable fort or forts, as a defense against our common enemy.

At a meeting held four days later, August 28, 1776, it was voted that

> ye three (3) field officers of ye regiment of this town be appointed as a committee to view the most

PLANS MADE BY SETTLERS

suitable places for building forts for ye defence of said town, and determine on some particular spot or place or places in each district for the purpose, and mark out the same.

It was further
(Recorded in Town Book of Wilkes-Barre.)

Voted that the above-said committee do recommend it to the people in each part as shall be set off by them to belong to any fort, to proceed forthwith in building said fort, etc., without either fee or reward from ye said town.

The committee appointed carefully considered the situation, and gave some time to the "study of the needs of each township." Sites were selected that offered the best positions for fortifications. Old forts erected some years before were repaired. Forty Fort and Pittston Fort were enlarged and strongly fortified.

The three field officers who were appointed a committee on the location of forts were members of the Twenty-fourth Regiment of Connecticut militia. This regiment which was organized a short time after the town of Westmoreland was established by an act of the Connecticut Legislature had as its purpose the defense of the town. The organization of this regiment, however, did not do much for the security of the settlement, as the members were all inhabitants of the Valley where every man was required to arm himself, "and in case of alarms or appearance of an enemy, stand for the defence of the town without further orders." The regiment was made up of nine small companies.

On August 23, 1776, the day before the meeting in the Wilkes-Barre District, Congress, in response to the settlers' appeal for aid,

Resolved, that two companies on the Continental Establishment be raised in the Town of Westmoreland, and stationed in proper places for the defence of the inhabitants of said Town, and parts adjacent, till further order of Congress; the commissioned officers of said two companies to be immediately appointed by Congress. That the pay of the men, to be raised as aforesaid, commence when they are armed and mustered, and that they be liable to serve in any part of the United States when ordered by Congress.

Congress appointed Robert Durkee and Samuel Ransom captains of the above-mentioned companies. The officers immediately set about getting recruits, and in less than two months the number in each company amounted to eighty-four men, or one hundred sixty-eight in all. They were called the "Two Independent Companies of Westmoreland." The settlers now felt safer when assured of this long-looked-for protection. This feeling of security, however, was not of long duration. The problems confronting Congress were too great to be handled by the soldiers available on the battleground, and on December 12, 1776, the "Two Independent Companies of Westmoreland" were ordered "to join General Washington with all possible expedition." With the withdrawal of these two companies, Wyoming suffered the temporary loss of her able-bodied young men. The flower of young manhood in the Valley, on whom the oldest and youngest depended for protection, made up the two companies. The dangers of attack increased as the Wyoming Valley was now a practically unprotected frontier.

That the fires of patriotism burned in the hearts of the Yankee settlers in the Wyoming Valley with a fierce intensity is proven by the fact that Wyoming

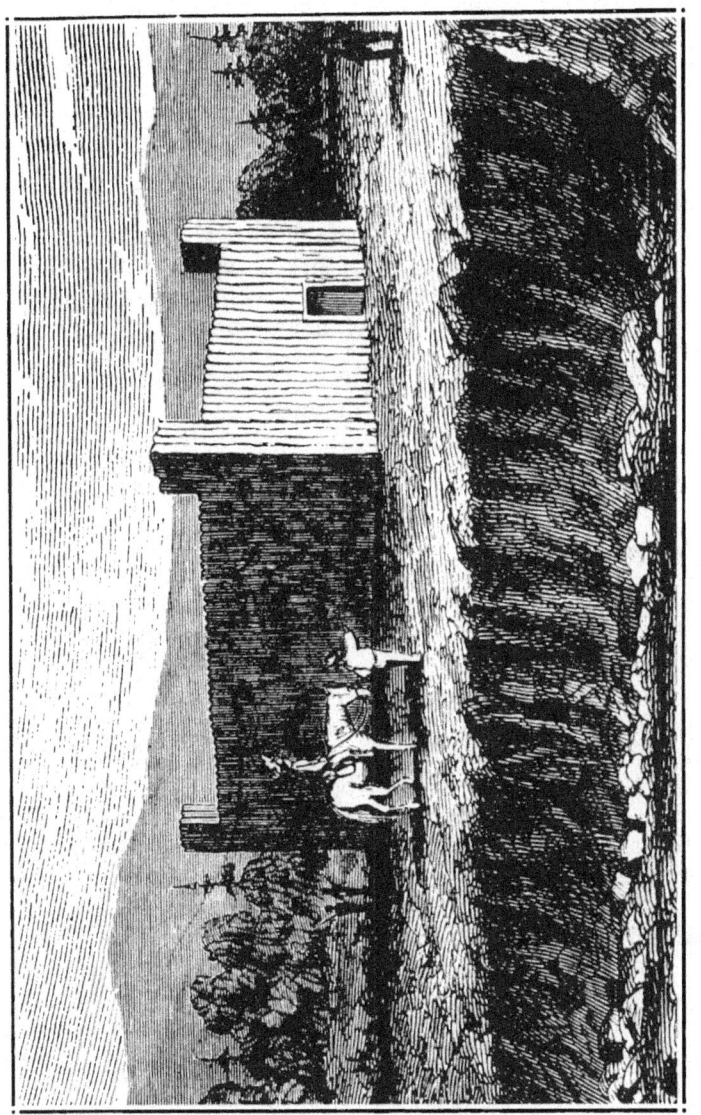

FORTY FORT

PLANS MADE BY SETTLERS 81

sent out two hundred men to help in the fight for freedom while her quota was only about twenty-one.

With the departure of the two companies from the Valley, many duties fell to the lot of those who were either too old or too young to enlist in the army and join in the fight for liberty. In addition to the many duties of the farmer, there was guard duty without intermission. Scouts were ever on the watch for the approach of the enemy. Then, too, there was the work of building forts. Despite the absence of the able-bodied, the work of erecting forts went on and all were completed and ready for occupancy before July, 1778.

BUILDING OF FORTS FOR THE PROTECTION OF THE INHABITANTS OF THE VALLEY

In compliance with the vote of the meeting held August 28, 1776, the settlers began the erection of forts for the protection of the inhabitants of the Valley.

WINTERMOOT'S FORT ERECTED PREVIOUS TO THE TOWN MEETING

One fort had been erected previous to the meeting of August 28th. It was called Wintermoot's, and was built by a family of that name. They had lived in the Valley for some time, but their loyalty was questioned, and they were looked upon with suspicion by the settlers in Wyoming. Many thought they were Tories who kept the British enemy posted about conditions in the settlement. This fort was situated in the upper end of the Valley on the west side of the river, and its erection had not been sanctioned by any person in authority. This circumstance only helped to increase suspicion in the hearts of the neighbors, who armed themselves not for the protection of their families alone, but for the protection of every man, woman, and child in the Valley, together with their possessions.

To protect themselves against a repetition of this unfortunate condition, it was ordered at the meeting of August, 1776, that all sites for forts should be selected by the committee appointed. By this arrangement it would be impossible for any person under suspicion to build a fort.

JENKINS' FORT

The site of this fort was selected by the committee a short time after the meeting, and the work of building it was started at once. This fort stood about a mile above Wintermoot's at the western extremity of the Fort Jenkins Bridge in Pittston.

The structure was a stockade built around and in "connection with the dwelling house of John Jenkins. The stockade was built by planting upright timbers in a trench of proper depth. These uprights were sharpened at the tops and fastened together by pins of wood and stiffened with two rows of timbers put on horizontally and pinned to the uprights inside, thus stiffening and uniting the whole into a substantial structure."

This fortification was built on the high bank of the river. A part of this bank has been washed away, and a large part of the site now lies in the bed of the river. The west side entrance to the new Fort Jenkins Bridge no doubt covers some of the location.

FORTY FORT

The inhabitants of the town of Kingston now began to rebuild Forty Fort under the direction of the committee. This fort was originally built in 1770, and was named for the first forty settlers who arrived in the Valley from Connecticut. It was now enlarged and strongly fortified.

The walls of this fort were of logs set upright in a trench five feet deep, rising to a height of twelve feet above the ground. The logs were sharpened at the top. Another row of logs placed in the same position against the first row protected the cracks between the logs in the first row. This arrangement formed a double wall insuring greater security to the inmates. Inside the walls huts were built to shelter the settlers. In times of attack the roofs of these buildings could be used by the garrison to protect the fort. Two gateways opened into the fortification, one from the north and one from the south. Sentry towers were placed at the four corners. Water was secured by the occupants from a spring located at the foot of the bank on which the fort stood. A sunken passageway led to this spring.

WILKES-BARRE FORT

The erection of this fort on the public square was begun in 1776, but it was not completed until 1778. The courthouse and jail of Westmoreland County were located within its walls, which, like Forty Fort, were composed of a double row of logs. The walls of this fort reached a height of sixteen feet above the ground. A gateway opened toward the river. Loopholes were provided in the walls so that in case of attack the garrison could protect itself without being exposed to the fire of the enemy. As at Forty Fort, shelter was provided inside the walls of the fort for the inmates. A trench surrounded the fort.

SHAWNEE FORT

Shawnee Fort was built on a hill south of Plymouth. The site was selected by the committee appointed for that purpose.

PITTSTON FORT

The erection of this fort on the east bank of the river almost opposite Fort Jenkins was started in 1772 under the approval of the proprietors. On May 20, 1772, a meeting of the proprietors was held at Wilkes-Barre. At this meeting it was voted

> that ye proprietors belonging to ye Town of Pittston have ye liberty to go into their town, and there to forty-fie and keep in a body near together, and Guard by themselves until further notice from this Committee.

This fort was built in the form of a triangle, and was composed of thirty-five houses "so constructed as to communicate from the one to the other in the upper story." It was a large fortification well and strongly built. Although the building of this fort was begun in 1772, it was not completed until about seven years later.

NINTH DAY

Grandmother had been busy all morning looking up her story for the ninth day and preparing questions on the lesson of the previous day. Now you try and answer them.

> When did the Indians return to the Valley?
> Were they friendly to the settlers?

CAPITULATION TABLE

PLANS MADE BY SETTLERS 85

To whom did the inhabitants of the Wyoming Valley appeal for help?

When they failed to get help, what did they do?

What did the settlers decide to do at the meetings held August 24 and 28, 1776, at Wilkes-Barre?

Who were the members of the committee appointed?

What did Congress resolve on August 23, 1776?

Who were appointed captains of the "Two Independent Companies of Westmoreland"?

When were these two companies ordered to join General Washington?

In what position was the Wyoming Valley placed by the withdrawal of these troops?

How many men did Wyoming send out to help in the fight for freedom?

By whom was Wintermoot's Fort built? Tell what you know about this fort.

Where was Jenkins' Fort? Describe it.

When was Forty Fort first erected? Describe it.

Where was Wilkes-Barre Fort located? Was this fort important?

Did Plymouth have a fort? Name it.

Locate Pittston Fort. How long did it take to build this fort? Of how many houses was it composed? Why was this fort started in 1772?

IX

DEATH OF THE HARDINGS AND HADSALLS

In June, 1778, scouting parties sent out by the settlers reported that Tories and Indians were quartered in the vicinity of Tunkhannock. The inhabitants of the Valley fled to the protection the forts afforded. During the day the men and boys of the colony proceeded to their farms which they continued to cultivate, returning to the shelter of the forts at night.

Unaware of the proximity of the enemy a number of the settlers, who were living in Jenkins' Fort, rode a distance of seven miles up the river to work their farms. Among them were Benjamin, Stukley, and Stephen Harding, Jr., who worked on the Harding farm. During the day all was peaceful and they were not molested. Toward evening, on June 30th, two Tories came to them and advised them to call off their guards as there was no danger of attack. The Hardings were immediately on the alert, and Stephen went to get their horses to hurry their return to the fort. Fearing their prey would escape, the two spies left at once to communicate with the Indians and Tories who were secreted near by.

Before Stephen returned his brothers had stopped working and made their way toward the river. In a ravine a short distance from the river bank the Indians awaited their coming and when they reached that point the unsuspecting victims were fired upon by the enemy. Benjamin and Stukley Harding fell and were cruelly put to death. John Gardner, who was with them, was taken prisoner.

On the adjoining farm James Hadsall and two men who were working with him were made prisoners. James Hadsall, Jr., returning from the island near by, was shot as he ascended the bank of the river. Two men who were with him escaped and fled to the woods. John Hadsall, a young brother of James, Jr., remained behind to fasten the boat and hid in the bushes when he heard the firing. He was the first of the ill-fated party to reach the fort, arriving there after midnight.

James Hadsall, Sr., the two men captured with him, and John Gardner were taken up Sutton's Creek where they were subjected to the most dreadful torture and put to death.

Stephen Harding, Jr., and the three others who escaped reached the fort the next morning.

Of the three Hardings who had gone out to work that morning, two were killed and one returned to the fort. Of the Hadsalls who worked on the adjoining farm, one was killed, one captured, and, after being brutally tortured, put to death, and one returned to the safety of the fort.

When the news of these horrible murders spread through the Valley, the hearts of the settlers were filled with sorrow, terror, and a desire to punish the perpetrators of this fiendish crime.

On the morning of the day following the murders, July 1, 1778, with Colonel Zebulon Butler, back from the Continental Army, Colonel Nathan Denison, and Lieutenant Colonel George Dorrance, both militia officers, at their head, the settlers marched from Forty Fort to the farm in Exeter where the bodies of the Hardings lay. This farm is now known as "Triple Springs Farm," and is owned by State Senator P. F. Joyce, of Pittston, who, in 1912, donated the plot of ground there on which the D. A. R. erected a marker in memory of Benjamin and Stukley Harding. This memorial was set up just one hundred and thirty-four years after the death of the Hardings.

When the settlers arrived at their destination they found two Indians watching the bodies, no doubt awaiting the arrival of other victims. They were shot by the settlers.

After securing the bodies of the Hardings the colonists returned, sad and disheartened, to Jenkins' Fort. The Hardings rest in Jenkins Cemetery, West Pittston.

INDIANS MAKE THEIR APPEARANCE IN VALLEY. WINTERMOOT'S FORT SURRENDERS. JENKINS' FORT TAKEN. BATTLE AND MASSACRE. TERMS OF CAPITULATION. INDIANS PLUNDER AND BURN THE SETTLEMENT. YANKEES FLEE IN TERROR. MAJOR BUTLER WITHDRAWS TROOPS

On the evening of the same day, July 1, 1778, the enemy made their appearance in the Valley. Wintermoot's Fort, under the command of Lieut. Elisha Scovell, surrendered on their approach. Major Butler, in command of the British Regulars, Tories and Indians, made this fort his headquarters during his stay in the Valley. The terms of surrender were as follows:

Wintermoot's Fort, July 1, 1778.

Art. 1. That Lieut. Elisha Scovell surrender the fort, with all the stores, arms and ammunition that are in said fort, as well public as private, to Major John Butler.

2. That the garrison shall not bear arms during the present contest and Major John Butler promises the men, women and children shall not be hurt, either by Indians or Rangers.

Almost immediately after taking possession of Fort Wintermoot, a detachment commanded by Captain Caldwell, of the Royal Greens marched on Fort Jenkins and demanded the surrender of that Fort. The garrison was made up of only eight men, who were unable to show any resistance. The terms of capitulation were as follows:

Fort Jenkins, July 1, 1778.
Between Major John Butler, on behalf of his Majesty King George the Third, and John Jenkins.

Art. 1. That the fort, with all the stores, arms and ammunition, be delivered up immediately.

2. That Major John Butler shall preserve to them intire the lives of the men, women and children.

With the surrender of Jenkins' Fort Major John Butler, in command of about eleven hundred men, had possession of the two forts on the west side of the river in the upper end of the Valley. The settlers, terrified by possibilities of attack by their fiendish enemies, hurried to the protection of the other forts in the Valley. Major John Butler now turned his covetous eyes toward Forty Fort, which the settlers were preparing to defend.

Col. Zebulon Butler was placed in command of the garrison at Forty Fort, which Chapman tells us numbered three hundred sixty-eight men. These were old men and young boys who were either too aged or too youthful to be accepted for service in the Continental Army. The able-bodied men were fighting for the liberty of the Colonies, far away from their homes and the loved ones in Wyoming.

The invaders now began plundering the Valley. Determined to drive them out of the settlement and unaware of the strength and number of the enemy, the little band of settlers marched to meet them July 3, 1778.

Three miles above Forty Fort they formed in line and made ready to charge the Tories and Indians. The settlers were under the command of Col. Zebulon Butler, Major John Garrett, Col. Denison and Lieut. Col. George Dorrance. The enemy was under the command of Major John Butler and Captains Pawling and Hopkins.

The settlers advanced on the enemy, pouring in a steady fire, which was returned. The enemy continued to fall back, the settlers pushing on until they found themselves in a clear space exposed to the fire of the merciless invaders.

While in this position they were attacked by the Indians who swooped down on them. Lieut. Col. George Dorrance received a mortal wound. Major John Garrett was killed. So terrible was the slaughter that the survivors fled from the battlefield. Every captain of a company fell. Of all the captains who had led their men forth to battle with high hopes and spirits not one returned to the fort alive.

Now began the terrible massacre. The Indians, with an insatiable thirst for blood, pursued the fleeing patriots and cut off their retreat to the fort. Unable to reach Forty Fort they fled to the river and some of them succeeded in reaching Monockonock Island. Others were fortunate enough to reach the other bank and fled to the fort at Wilkes-Barre. Many were taken prisoners. To these no mercy was shown.

Sixteen of the prisoners were tied in a circle around

HARDINGS AND HADSALLS 91

a rock and after being tortured by the Indians fourteen were put to death by Queen Esther, a half-breed, who dashed out their brains with a tomahawk. The other two succeeded in freeing themselves from their bonds and escaped to the woods. This rock is known as "Queen Esther's Rock" and is situated along the river road at Wyoming just above the new bridge crossing the river at that place. It is covered by a grating to prevent tourists from chipping off pieces for souvenirs.

During the night the settlers managed the escape of Colonel Butler from the Valley so that he could continue helping General Washington in the Colonies' fight for liberty. Had he remained in Forty Fort he would have had to sign the articles of capitulation and that would have prevented him from taking up arms against England again during the war.

Col. Denison, who survived the massacre, now took command of the remainder of the garrison at Forty Fort. When the surrender of the fort was demanded the next day the settlers submitted, knowing that further resistance was useless, and the enemy was allowed to take possession on the following terms:

Westmoreland, July 4, 1778.

Capitulation made and completed between Major John Butler, on behalf of his Majesty King George the Third, and Colonel Nathan Denison, of the United States of America.

Art. 1. That the inhabitants of the settlement lay down their arms and the garrisons be demolished.

2. That the inhabitants are to occupy their farms peaceably and the lives of the inhabitants preserved entire and unhurt.

3. That the continental stores be delivered up.

4. That Major John Butler will use his utmost influence that the private property of the inhabitants shall be preserved entire to them.

5. That the prisoners in Forty Fort be delivered up and that Samuel Finch, now in Major Butler's possession, be delivered up also.

6. That the property taken from the people called Tories up the river be made good and they to remain in peaceable possession of their farms, unmolested in a free trade in and throughout this State as far as lies in my power.

7. That the inhabitants that Colonel Denison now capitulates for, together with himself, do not take up arms during the present contest.'

The articles of surrender could not be signed within the walls of Forty Fort and so the capitulation took place on the neutral ground of the near-by cabin of Mrs. Bennett. The table on which the articles were signed may be seen today in the rooms of the Wyoming Historical and Geological Society on South Franklin Street, Wilkes-Barre. Here also may be seen the signatures of many of the patriots who took part in the Battle of Wyoming.

The terms of capitulation having been accepted by the settlers, Major Butler, at the head of his British Provincials and Tories and accompanied by his savage allies, approached the fort to the music of fife and drum and with banners flying. The gates were thrown open by the settlers. Butler and his party entered by the north gate while the Indians marched through the south gate. The arms of the settlers were stacked in the center of the fort and surrendered to Major Butler, who at once turned them over to the savages.

The Indians now proceeded to rob the inmates of

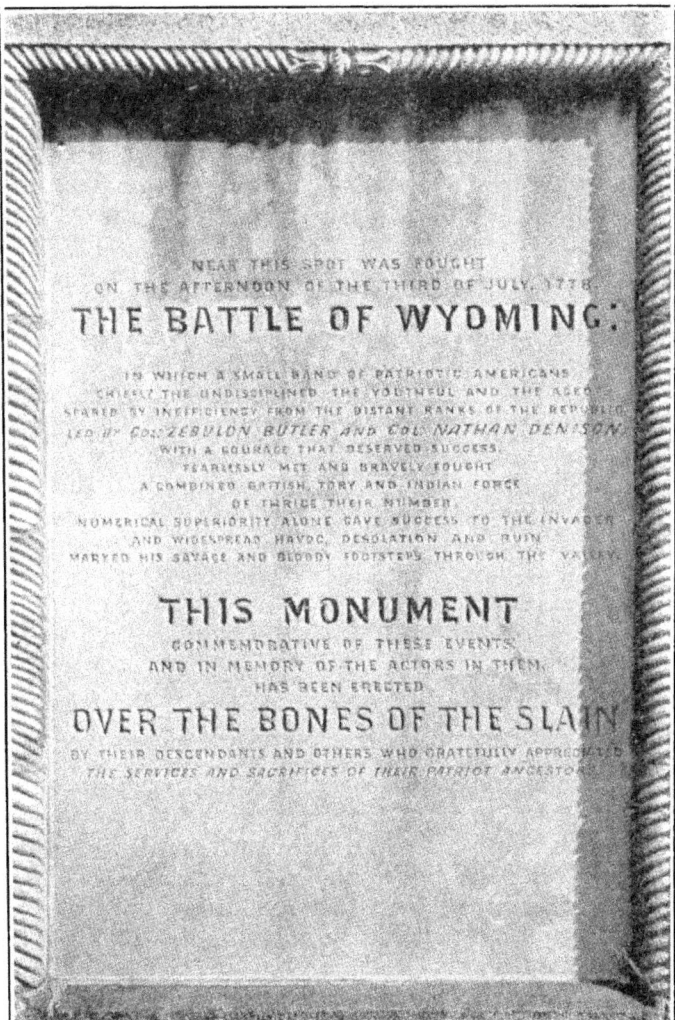

TABLET

the fort of their movable possessions, even the clothes they wore. After possessing themselves of everything available in the fort the savages, crazed with success and victory, plundered the Valley, leaving destruction and desolation behind them.

The surviving inhabitants fled from the Valley in terror. Many died from hunger and exposure to the elements. Some were lost and never reached their destination, while others met death in the swamps through which they fled. So dreadful was the death toll that the swamps have since been known as the "Shades of Death."

Major Butler withdrew his forces from the Valley a few days later. He was accompanied by some of his savage allies, but many remained to plunder the settlement and terrorize the remaining inhabitants.

Captain Spalding, of the Continental Army, who had been sent by the Colonial Government at the head of a company for the relief of Wyoming, met the settlers fleeing through the swamps. The presence of the soldiers assured some protection to the fleeing Yankees. Upon learning that the Valley was in possession of the enemy, Captain Spalding discontinued his march and rendered all help possible to the fugitives. He then returned to the Delaware to await further orders.

The Battle of Wyoming, one of the three battles of the Revolutionary War fought on the soil of our State, was the turning point of the Colonies' fight for liberty. When the news of the dreadful massacre of the inhabitants of the Wyoming Valley reached England, the English people were so incensed that they rose up as a body in protest and the King found it impossible to get more recruits for the English Army in his own land and had to hire soldiers to go on with the war against the Colonies.

94 PIONEER DAYS IN WYOMING VALLEY

YANKEE SETTLERS RETURN TO VALLEY. FORTIFY THEMSELVES ON SOUTH MAIN STREET, WILKES-BARRE. HARTLEY'S EXPEDITION. ATTACK BY THE INDIANS. MARAUDING PARTIES IN VALLEY.

On August 4, 1778, Colonel Zebulon Butler, with Captain Spalding and his company, returned to Wilkes-Barre and took possession of the once thriving settlement. They found the Valley overrun with Indians and established themselves in a log house on South Main Street, which they fortified. They then went about the work of rebuilding Fort Wyoming. A number of the settlers had returned to the Valley and some of them assisted the soldiers in rebuilding the fort.

A large body of Indians occupied the settlement of Sheshequin (near Towanda) in Westmoreland. This location had furnished a convenient base for supplies for the Indians during their attacks on the Yankee settlement. Colonel Hartley, of the Pennsylvania line, stationed at Muncy Fort on the West Branch, was ordered to move against Sheshequin in September, 1778, and after being reinforced by a company from the Wyoming Valley the attack was made. Many of the Indians were killed in the battle which followed. Colonel Hartley also suffered the loss of some of his men and a larger number were wounded. The expedition was a successful one, the Indian village was destroyed and Queen Esther's castle burned. Captain Spalding and the men under his command were eulogized in Colonel Hartley's report for the bravery displayed on this occasion.

For more than three months following the massacre the bodies of the dead settlers lay on the battlefield exposed to the ravages of the elements.

On the morning of October 28, 1778, Lieutenant

HARDINGS AND HADSALLS

John Jenkins and a force of armed men proceeded to the scene of battle to bury the bodies of their fallen neighbors. They brought with them two carts on which to carry the dead. When they reached a point about half-way to the battleground the carts were filled with dead bodies. Here they dug a hole and, with heavy hearts, placed the bodies in it. Many more bodies were found later and all placed in this common grave.

Near this spot now stands the Wyoming Monument, where, on December 5, 1833, the bones of eighty-three skeletons were placed in the monument vault. The monument is sixty-two feet six inches high.

During the early part of November the Indians swooped down on the settlements along the Susquehanna, but were repulsed at Wyoming by Colonel Butler and his men.

Many attacks were made during the winter months and on March 21, 1779, a large body of Tories and Indians tried to storm the fort. The garrison succeeded in driving them away. Defeated in their attempt to get possession of the fort they set about destroying the property of the settlers. Horses and cattle were seized and driven away by the Indians. Other domestic animals were shot by them and left to die. Among the buildings to which they applied the torch were five barns containing hay and grain and ten houses that had been deserted by the inhabitants.

Marauding parties of Indians continued to infest the Valley. The mountains surrounding Wyoming afforded them shelter and provided an unobstructed view of the settlement, but gave no hint to the Yankees of the danger lurking in the forests. The Indians, with their native cunning, continued to steal out when the opportunity afforded itself and, after accomplishing their purpose, skulked back to the friendly shelter of the mountains.

TENTH DAY

Grandmother was hardly prepared for the enthusiasm of the children on the tenth day. They were anxious to hear again every detail of the lesson of the previous day and were very proud of the fact that their home (the farm on which the Hardings were killed by the Indians) held an important place in the history of the Wyoming Valley.

After answering many questions, Grandmother finally succeeded in asking hers, which are as follows:

What report was made by the scouting parties sent out by the settlers in 1778?
Did the settlers continue to cultivate their lands?
Tell the story of the Hardings.
Tell what you know about the Hadsalls.
How many men were tortured and put to death?
How many returned to Fort Jenkins alive?
How did the settlers feel about this terrible crime?
What did they do the following day?
Is there a marker on this spot?
Where are the Hardings buried?
When did the enemy make their appearance in the Valley?
What fort surrendered first?
When did Fort Jenkins capitulate?
What were the terms of surrender?
With the surrender of Fort Jenkins, what part of the Wyoming Valley did Major Butler have in his possession?
How many men were under his command?
Who was in command of the garrison at Forty Fort?

WYOMING MONUMENT

HARDINGS AND HADSALLS 97

How many men and boys made up this garrison?
Were they able-bodied men?
What did the enemy do now?
When did the settlers march to meet the invaders?
Where did they form in line for battle?
Name the officers in command of the settlers.
Who commanded the British, Tories and Indians?
Tell what you know about the Battle of Wyoming.
Tell what you know about the terrible massacre that followed the battle.
What did the brutal Queen Esther do?
Where is Queen Esther's Rock?
Why were the settlers anxious to get Col. Zebulon Butler out of the Valley?
When did Forty Fort surrender? What were the terms?
Where were the articles of capitulation signed?
What society has possession of the table on which the surrender was signed?
Where may it be seen?
After the settlers had accepted the terms of capitulation, what did Major Butler do?
Did he control the Indians so as to protect the settlers after the fort surrendered?
Tell about the flight of the settlers from the Valley.
When did Major Butler withdraw his troops?
By whom were the settlers aided in their flight?
What battle was the turning point of the Revolutionary War?
When did Colonel Zebulon Butler, with Captain Spalding and his company, return to the Wyoming Valley?
Where did they establish themselves?
Who assisted the soldiers in rebuilding Fort Wyoming?

What was the purpose of the expedition under Colonel Hartley sent against Sheshequin?

Where is this town located?

Was this expedition a success?

When were the bodies of the settlers, who had fallen during the Battle of Wyoming and the Wyoming Massacre, buried?

Where do the bones of the victims now repose?

Tell me something about the Wyoming Monument.

Tell what you know about the attacks of the Indians during the winter of 1778-1779.

X

THE STORY OF FRANCES SLOCUM

Almost every child of school age in the Wyoming Valley is familiar with the story of Frances Slocum.

Jonathan Slocum, a native of Rhode Island, with his wife and family, emigrated to the Wyoming Valley in 1777. He took up land in Wilkes-Barre on which he settled and built his house on the plot of ground now occupied by the Frances Slocum Playground.

One day in November, 1778, while the men of the family were at work in the fields, four Indians attacked the house where there were at the time, besides Mrs. Slocum and four of her children, two boys named Kingsley and a colored girl.

The Kingsley boys were just outside the door sharpening a knife, but so noiseless was the approach of the savages that the first intimation that the family had of their presence was when the older of the Kingsley boys was shot down by one of the Indians, who proceeded to scalp him with the knife he had been sharpening.

Mrs. Slocum and the children were terror stricken. The oldest daughter, a child of nine years, seized her little two-year-old brother and ran out the back door toward the fort. She presented such a picture of terror that the Indians, laughing uproariously, let her go. They then seized one of the Slocum boys who was lame, but Mrs. Slocum pleaded with them to let him go and showed them how difficult it was for him to walk. They finally released him. Little Frances, who was then only four years old, next fell into their clutches, together with the remaining Kingsley boy and the colored girl. The distracted mother begged them to leave her little girl, but, ignoring her plea, they hurried off to the shelter of the mountains.

In a few minutes this peaceful home was transformed into a house of mourning. The alarm was given immediately, but the Indians moved with such rapidity and cunning that not a trace of them could be found.

A month later another attack was made on the Slocum family while they were at work a short distance from the house. Mr. Slocum was shot and his aged father-in-law was wounded and then killed. Both were scalped. William, the son, was shot in the leg, but succeeded in reaching the house. Today, after the lapse of almost one hundred and fifty years, we must still sympathize with this sorrowing wife and mother, who in such a short space of time saw her little daughter carried off by the Indians and both her husband and father killed and scalped by fiendish savages.

While Mrs. Slocum lived the hope of again seeing her dear one was ever in her heart. Her sons made several trips through the West and up into Canada, hoping to get a trace of their lost sister, but all proved unsuccessful.

In 1807, twenty-nine years after she had lost her little girl, Mrs. Slocum died. The brothers never gave up the search, and after sixty years their perseverance was rewarded.

In 1835 Colonel Ewing, of Indiana, a United States agent, while on a business trip that brought him far from the hustle and bustle of city streets, tired and weary, found himself at nightfall stranded on the bank of the Mississinewa, a tributary of the Wabash. His horse was almost exhausted and unable to push on;

FRANCES SLOCUM

he looked about for a habitation where he could spend the night. Finding himself near an Indian village called "Deaf-men's Village," he sought shelter at a prosperous-looking cabin. He was hospitably received and given refreshments and a place to sleep.

The family retired for the night, but the mother, a very old woman, continued to busy herself about the cabin. Colonel Ewing, while observing her about her work, noticed that her hair was light, and that the skin that showed from beneath her dress was white. Suspecting that she was a white woman, he began to question her.

She readily acknowledged that she was a white woman. She told him that she had been stolen by the Indians when she was a small girl. She could not remember the name of the town in which she lived at the time she was carried away by the Indians, but she did remember her father's name was Slocum, and that they lived on the banks of the Susquehanna River.

In the hope that some of her family were still alive, Colonel Ewing, on his return home, wrote a letter to the postmaster in Lancaster, Pa., and requested that the letter be published. For some reason the letter was put aside, and was not published until two years later. A few days after its publication the paper in which it appeared fell into the hands of one of Frances' brothers who lived in Wilkes-Barre.

And in 1838, just sixty years after Frances had been stolen by the Indians, her two brothers and her sister traveled to Indiana, and there in an Indian cabin found their long-lost sister, now an old woman, and the queen of her tribe. They readily identified her by an injury she had received to the first finger of one of her hands before she was stolen by the Indians. She could not speak English, and had no idea of her age. Her husband, who had been a chief of the tribe, was dead.

102 PIONEER DAYS IN WYOMING VALLEY

The brothers and sister pleaded with Frances to return with them, but she refused. She had pledged herself to remain with the Indians when her husband was dying, and she would not break her promise to him. She was happy with her two daughters, a son-in-law, and three grandchildren. Her Indian name was "Ma-con-a-qua," and she had all the characteristics of the Indian, but there was a dignity about her that distinguished her from the other women of the tribe.

And so, after sixty years, Frances Slocum was found by her family, but nothing could induce her to return to civilization. She had lived so long with the Indians that she knew no other life, and it was too late to transplant her to the banks of the Susquehanna, the home of her early childhood.

REINFORCEMENTS ARRIVE IN WYOMING. COLONEL BUTLER DRIVES LURKING INDIANS OUT OF VALLEY. GENERAL SULLIVAN'S EXPEDITION. INDIAN POWER BROKEN

Hope again came to life in the hearts of the settlers when, during the early part of April, 1779, a regiment of three hundred men arrived in Wyoming. With the help of this force, Colonel Butler was able to drive the lurking Indians out of the Valley. On April 20th Major Powell arrived in Wyoming with a battalion of two hundred men under his command. These two forces had been ordered to Wyoming, there to await the arrival of General Sullivan and his army. The forces, under the command of General Sullivan, were then to march against the Six Nations and drive them out of their stronghold. General Sullivan arrived in the Valley two months later, on June 23rd, and the combined forces began their march against the Indians on July 31, 1779.

THE STORY OF FRANCES SLOCUM 103

The departure of General Sullivan and his army from the Valley must have been an imposing spectacle. One hundred and twenty boats were propelled up the river by soldiers accompanied by a guard of troops. Two thousand horses, carrying provisions for the army, moved along the eastern shore of the river. This part of the expedition, we are told, was six miles in length. Many of the Indians still lurked in the mountains, and terror must have filled their hearts as they looked down from their hiding places on this expedition that had as its object the breaking of the Indian power forever in the Wyoming Valley.

The enemy had taken up their position behind a breastwork they had erected at Newtown on the Tioga River near the present city of Elmira. It was at this place that General Sullivan attacked them on August 29th. They were driven out of their position and fled in confusion. No attempt was made by the Indians to stay the progress of the avenging army. Proceeding into the Indian country, they destroyed eighteen Indian villages, and desolated the country as far as the Genessee River. The Indians now found themselves in the position they had many times forced upon the unsuspecting settlers.

So vigorous was General Sullivan's campaign that the power so long held by the Six Nations was broken. There was no longer any reason to fear their marauding expeditions. The army returned by way of Tioga Point and arrived at Wyoming on October 7, 1779. Three days later General Sullivan, with his army, departed for Easton.

Colonel Butler remained in command of the garrison at Wyoming. Many of the settlers, relieved of the fear of Indian attacks, returned to the Valley. The town was rebuilt and soon the settlement was in a flourishing condition.

A few articles relating to the time of General Sullivan's expedition may be seen in the building of the Wyoming Historical and Geological Society, Wilkes-Barre.

ELEVENTH DAY

Who was Frances Slocum?

When was she stolen by the Indians?

When and how were her father and grandfather killed?

How many years elapsed before her family found her?

Tell all you know about the story of Frances Slocum.

What stirred up hope in the hearts of the settlers in the early part of 1779?

What can you tell me about General Sullivan's expedition?

Did he break the Indian power?

When did General Sullivan return to Wyoming?

What colonel was in command of the garrison after General Sullivan departed from the Wyoming Valley?

Did any of the settlers return to Wyoming?

Where may some of the things relating to General Sullivan's expedition be seen?

XI

CONTROVERSY BETWEEN PENNSYLVANIA AND CONNECTICUT BEGINS ANEW

The controversy between Pennsylvania and Connecticut over the right to the Wyoming Valley now began anew, and was referred to Congress. That body appointed a Board of Commissioners to meet at Trenton in 1782, and hear both sides of the controversy. The committee, after carefully considering the claims of Connecticut and Pennsylvania, handed down the following decision:

This cause has been well argued by the Learned Council on both sides. The Court are now to pronounce their Sentence or Judgment.

We are unanimously of the opinion that the State of Connecticut has no right to the Lands in Controversy.

We are also unanimously of Opinion that the Jurisdiction and pre-emption of all the territory lying within the Charter boundary of Pennsylvania and now claimed by the State of Connecticut, do of right belong to the State of Pennsylvania.

(Signed)
William Whipple,
Welcome Arnold,
Dav'd Brearly,
Cyrus Griffin,
William C. Houston.

Trenton, December 30, 1782.

106 PIONEER DAYS IN WYOMING VALLEY

The Connecticut settlers, believing that the decision related to the government and did not affect the right of soil, agreeably submitted to the decision of the Court.

Writing for the commissioners, January 1, 1783, Cyrus Griffin advised President Dickinson that they recommended

> that the settlers should be quieted in all their claims by an act of the Pennsylvania Assembly; and that the right of soil as derived from Connecticut should be held sacred.

On January 6, 1783, President Dickinson issued a proclamation. All Pennsylvania claimants were prohibited from interfering in any way with any persons who had settled in the Wyoming Valley under the authority of the Connecticut Colony until the Legislature had made laws and "passed judgment in such case." In an appeal to Congress, under date of January 18, 1783, the settlers, as citizens of Pennsylvania, begged the State of Pennsylvania to protect their rights.

The General Assembly now ordered two companies of Rangers, under the command of Captains Robinson and Shrawder, to proceed to Wyoming, where they were to maintain the post and protect the settlement. Captain Shrawder, with his company, arrived in the Valley on March 21st. He stationed his men in Wyoming Fort, to which he gave the name of Fort Dickinson in honor of the president of the Supreme Executive Council. Captain Robinson arrived later in the month, but was recalled soon after peace was declared with England.

On October 29th, Captain Christie arrived in command of a company. Now began a period of oppres-

CONTROVERSY BEGINS ANEW 107

sion for the Yankee settlers who had already suffered so much. The soldiers, with nothing to do, became rude and insolent, and instead of protecting the settlers and their possessions, subjected the Yankees to persecutions that would drive them to acts of violence.

THE ICE FLOOD OF 1784. APPEAL FOR HELP MADE TO THE GENERAL ASSEMBLY. SECOND PENNAMITE-YANKEE WAR. DEATH OF ELISHA GARRETT AND CHESTER PIERCE. JOHN FRANKLIN DEMANDS SURRENDER OF FORT

Amid terrible suffering under the jurisdiction of the merciless soldiers, the spring of 1784 opened with a sudden thaw. On March 13th and 14th the Valley was flooded by a steady downpour of rain. On the 15th the ice began to break up, and the river rose rapidly. The inhabitants of the Valley hurried to the mountains for safety. Their sufferings were intense. Food was scarce and the soldiers plundered the settlement of all that the flood and storm had spared. President Dickinson appealed to the General Assembly for relief for the little colony, but they adjourned without taking action.

Under date of April 5, 1784, Robert Martin and John Franklin addressed the following memorial:

> To the Honorable the President, the Vice-President and Executive Council of Pennsylvania:
> That on the 15th day of March last the river Susquehanna rose into a flood exceeding all degrees ever before known, that its rise was so sudden as to give no time to guard against its mischief; that it swept away about one hundred and fifty (150) houses, with all the provisions, house furniture, farming tools and cattle of the owners, and gave

but just opportunity for the inhabitants to fly for their lives to the high ground; that by this dreadful calamity one thousand persons are left destitute of provisions, clothing and every means of life, and to add to the calamity, the Winter Crop of Grain on the Ground is so harrowed up by the ice as to be nearly ruined. Their deplorable case was laid before the Late Assembly for their consideration, but they adjourned without taking any resolution thereon.

Your Memorialists therefore pray that these suffering people may be recommended to publick charity or such other method for their relief may be adopted, as your wisdom shall devise and your Memorialists shall ever pray.

The General Assembly failed to harken to the appeals for help, and the soldiers continued their persecutions. At last, the settlers, finding it impossible to submit longer, resisted the authority of their oppressors.

On May 13 and 14, 1784, the soldiers dispossessed one hundred and fifty families, and drove them out of the Valley at the point of the bayonet. No consideration was given to age or sex. About five hundred men, women, and children were forced to travel through sixty miles of an almost pathless wilderness. Many died from exposure and lack of food.

The acts of violence committed by the soldiers were resented by the citizens throughout Pennsylvania. Everywhere sympathy was expressed for the unhappy settlers who had been driven from their homes. The General Assembly, who had refused to listen to the appeals of the inhabitants of Wyoming, could no longer disregard the conditions in the Valley, and a committee was appointed to visit Wyoming and make an in-

GEN. JOHN SULLIVAN

CONTROVERSY BEGINS ANEW 109

vestigation of the charges against the soldiers stationed there. The commissioners appointed were accompanied by the sheriff of Northumberland County. As a result of this investigation of the charges, the troops were discharged on June 15th with the exception of a few who were left to take care of Fort Dickinson.

A proclamation was issued, asking the settlers to return to their former homes in Wyoming, and assuring them protection on condition that they obey the laws of Pennsylvania.

Many of the soldiers by whom the settlers had been so brutally treated remained in the Valley and found employment with the Pennsylvania land claimants. For a time some of them lived in vacant houses in Kingston, and supported themselves by plundering the farms of the settlers. Later these men joined Justice of the Peace Patterson, who had assumed charge of the garrison in Fort Dickinson.

The Yankees, alarmed at the menace of the enlarged garrison in their midst, decided it was time to seek the protection of a fortified place. They accordingly garrisoned themselves at Forty Fort.

On July 20th a party of the settlers left Forty Fort to look over some fields of grain in the vicinity of Plymouth, about five miles from the fort. After proceeding for some distance, they were attacked by a party of Patterson's soldiers, who fired upon them. As a result of this attack two young men, Elisha Garrett and Chester Pierce, were killed. The remainder of the party reached Forty Fort in safety.

The settlement now became one general house of mourning. On every side Patterson and his followers were denounced for the murder of these promising youths. A meeting was held which was attended by every settler able to bear arms. A few days later the Yankees moved in a body from Forty Fort determined to get possession of Fort Dickinson and drive out their oppressors. Patterson had in some way learned of their plan and, with his garrison, was prepared to defend and hold the fort.

Failing in this move, the settlers marched to Mill Creek where they seized the mill which had been in possession of the Pennsylvania Party. This was the only mill in the Valley, and the seizure of it at this time was a lucky move on the part of the Yankees, as their food supply was low, for it afforded them an opportunity to grind sufficient wheat for the use of the garrison at Forty Fort.

The hearts of the settlers who had suffered so much from the merciless persecution of Patterson and his party were now filled with a desire for revenge. The repeated brutality of their oppressors only helped to make them more determined to protect their rights. With this end in view, they decided to lay siege to Fort Dickinson and surrounded the fort. Captain John Franklin was in command of the settlers. Captain Franklin despatched a note to the garrison demanding the surrender of the fort as follows:

Wyoming, July 27, 1784.

Gentlemen—In the name and behalf of the inhabitants of this place, who held their lands under the Connecticut claim, and were lately, without the law, or even the color of the law, driven from their possessions in a hostile and unconstitutional manner, we, in the name of these injured and incensed inhabitants, demand an immediate surrender of your garrison into our hands, together with our possessions and property, which if complied with, you shall be treated with humanity and commiseration, otherwise the consequences will prove fatal and bloody to every person found in the garrison.

CONTROVERSY BEGINS ANEW 111

We give you two hours for a decisive answer, and will receive the same at Mr. Bailey's.
(Signed) John Franklin,
in behalf of the injured.

News now spread through the Valley that magistrates were on their way from Northumberland, accompanied by troops to restore peace, and see that all the inhabitants of the Valley were given justice. The settlers, on receiving this information, abandoned their plan to take the fort and returned to their quarters at Forty Fort. Hoping for a peaceful settlement of their troubles, they awaited the arrival of the magistrates.

On the 29th of July, Commissioners Thomas Hewet, David Mead, and Robert Martin arrived in Wyoming. Conferences were held between the warring parties but they could not come to any agreement. On August 5th, letters were sent to both the Yankees and Pennamites, commanding them in the name of the Commonwealth to deliver up their arms, and such a number of men as the commissioners would consider proper to be put in charge of the high sheriff until the decision of the Chief Justice would be made known. The men not in custody were to be bound over to keep the peace. The settlers readily acceded to the demands of the commissioners, but the Pennamites refused to give up their arms. Being defied by Patterson and his followers, the commissioners permitted the Connecticut people to again take up their arms for self-defense, and requested the Supreme Executive Council of Pennsylvania to "come forward with the militia with as much despatch as possible."

During the early part of August, Colonel Armstrong arrived in the Valley in command of a force. He immediately issued a proclamation demanding the cessation of all hostilities and the surrender of the arms of both parties, promising that peace would again be restored, and all parties treated with justice. The Yankees, at first suspicious, hesitated about surrendering their arms, but on the repeated assurances of Armstrong that they would be given protection and justice, they allowed the soldiers to disarm them. They almost immediately realized that they had been betrayed by the men who had given their word of honor to protect them, as the Pennamits under the command of Patterson were allowed to keep their arms.

The Yankee settlers were now treacherously surrounded by Armstrong's men and made prisoners. Thirty were placed under the care of a strong guard and marched to Easton where they were imprisoned. About forty others were bound and sent under guard to the prison at Sunbury. A large number of the imprisoned men escaped and hurried back to the Valley. When they reached Wyoming, they were gratified to find reinforcements from Vermont awaiting them, and they at once took possession of Forty Fort determined to protect whatever remained of their harvest.

On September 20th, a party of Armstrong's men started to gather the harvest, when an attack by the settlers forced them to abandon their plunder and flee to the shelter of their fort. On Sunday night, September 25th, the settlers made an attack on the house in which Armstrong was stationed, but were driven back. Another attack was made on these quarters a few nights later, when Magistrates Reed and Henderson were killed while attempting to escape.

Colonel Armstrong left the Valley September 26th for Philadelphia to report to Council the situation at Wyoming in an effort to secure reinforcements to protect the Pennsylvania claimants. When the news of the attack in which Reed and Henderson were

CHEVALIER DE LA LUZERNE

CONTROVERSY BEGINS ANEW 113

killed reached Philadelphia, Colonel Armstrong was authorized to raise a force and proceed with them to the Wyoming Valley for the purpose of expelling the settlers from the disputed territory.

Armstrong found the task of raising a force much harder than he had anticipated. The majority of the inhabitants of Pennsylvania were beginning to look on the Wyoming settlers as a persecuted people, and would take no part in bearing arms against them. After many disappointments, Armstrong succeeded in raising a force of about one hundred men, and proceeded with them to Wyoming, arriving in the Valley October 17th. He remained in Wyoming for some time, awaiting the arrival of reinforcements, but as winter approached he realized that help was not coming, and, after discharging his force, returned to Philadelphia.

The Pennsylvania Party abandoned Fort Dickinson November 27, 1784, and it was destroyed by the settlers three days later. This was the last expedition fitted up by the State of Pennsylvania against the residents of the Wyoming Valley.

During 1785 and 1786 the settlers continued to cultivate and improve the land, and at the same time put forth every effort to secure a trial to decide the title to the territory.

COUNTY OF LUZERNE ESTABLISHED

Under date of September 25, 1786, Luzerne County was established by an act. The county was named in honor of the Chevalier de la Luzerne, then the Minister from France to the United States. (He was the first Minister from France to the United States.)

LAW PASSED BY GENERAL ASSEMBLY. SUSPENSION ACT. LAW REPEALED IN 1790. COMPROMISE ACT. CONTROVERSY AT AN END

On March 28, 1787, the General Assembly of the State of Pennsylvania passed a law known as "The Confirming Law of 1787." This law was for the purpose of

> ascertaining and confirming to certain persons called Connecticut Claimants the Lands by them claimed within the County of Luzerne, and for other purposes therein mentioned.

This law was suspended under date of March 29, 1788, by the "Suspension Act of 1788," and repealed under date of April 1, 1790.

Although Luzerne County was represented in the General Assembly, courts established, and laws executed by the settlers, the right of title was not decided until April 4, 1799, when the Compromise Act was passed, and a later law in 1801 compensating the Pennsylvania claimants by grants of land elsewhere, or an equivalent in cash, and confirming the titles of the Connecticut settlers with the understanding that they pay to the State of Pennsylvania a small sum per acre.

The controversy was at last at an end and the Wyoming Valley, her soil hallowed with the blood of many loved ones, enjoyed the peace sought by the first Yankee pioneers in the Valley.

TWELFTH DAY

The last day of the story had arrived, and it was with a feeling of regret that Grandmother began to

CONTROVERSY BEGINS ANEW 115

question her audience on the lesson of the previous day, as she had enjoyed reviewing the early history of the Valley as much as the children had enjoyed hearing it. See how well you can answer the questions.

Why did Congress appoint a Board of Commissioners to meet at Trenton in 1782?

What was the decision of this board?

Did the Connecticut settlers submit to the decision?

What proclamation did President Dickinson issue?

What action was taken by the General Assembly?

Did the soldiers give protection to the settlers?

Tell what you know about the ice flood of 1784, and conditions in the Wyoming Valley.

What appeal was made to the President, the Vice-President, and Executive Council of Pennsylvania?

Did they respond to the appeal of the settlers?

What did the soldiers do in May?

Did the inhabitants of Pennsylvania approve of this persecution of the settlers?

What action was taken by the General Assembly?

Tell about conditions in the Valley at this time.

What circumstances led up to the deaths of Elisha Garrett and Chester Pierce?

Were Patterson and his followers denounced by the settlers for these uncalled-for murders?

Tell about the attack on Fort Dickinson. Failing to take the fort, what did the settlers do next?

Tell about the attack on Fort Dickinson July 27th.

What good news was received by the settlers at this time?

What did the commissioners do after arriving in the Valley?

Did the Yankees and Pennamites co-operate with the commissioners?

Tell the story of the first traitor in the Valley, Colonel Armstrong.
How did he treat the settlers?
When was Luzerne County established?
What was the Confirming Law of 1787?
When was this law suspended? When repealed?
When was the Compromise Act passed?
Tell about the Compensation Act passed in 1801.
When did the controversy end?

EARLY MAP OF WYOMING

XII

THE END OF THE STORY

"Well, children," concluded Grandmother, "I have told you all I know about the early history of the Wyoming Valley, and as I feel some parts of my story have impressed you more than others, I want you to tell me what part of the history of the Valley has interested you most.

"I am going to begin with Frances. Can you tell Grandmother what you liked best, dear?"

"Oh! Grandmother, I liked Frances Slocum best," replied Frances. "She was just as old as I am when the Indians stole her away. I am glad the Indians don't live up in our woods, because if they did they might steal other little girls."

"That is very true," replied Grandmother, "and I am glad, too, dear. Now, Joe, I would like to hear what part of the story interested you most."

"Why, Grandmother, it has all been so interesting that I don't know how to begin," replied Joe. "It is the first time I ever heard about the ancient fortifications in the Valley. The story about the grasshopper war in the Indian history of the Valley was very interesting, and I liked the story about the first white man who visited the Valley."

"Grandmother, I know something, too," George interrupted. "The first settlement and the massacre of the first settlers."

Mary Patricia wanted Grandmother to know that she, too, was interested, and her choice of events was the bravery of Captain Ogden.

Frances, not to be outdone by the others, wondered if Grandmother would take her to see a little papoose some day.

Joe was enthusiastic over the defeat of Plunkett's expedition, and said he would like to see "Rampart Rocks." Frances wanted to see the playground where Frances Slocum lived and played when she was a little girl, and George thought he would like to visit Sheshequin.

Mary Patricia's suggestion was to read all the names on the Wyoming Monument, and then visit the building of the Wyoming Historical and Geological Society, and see the table on which the articles of capitulation were signed for the surrender of Forty Fort.

The lesson ended by Grandmother telling again the story of the Hardings and the Wyoming Massacre.

"Now, children," continued Grandmother, "we have finished the story of pioneer days, and just as soon as school is out, we will take up the parts that interest you most and go over them again before the beginning of the Sesqui-Centennial. And we will also visit all the points of historic interest in the Valley."

And so the story ends.

INDEX

Armstrong, Col., Arrives in Valley, 111-13
Butler, Col. Zebulon, 87, 89, 91
Capitulation at Forty Fort, 91
Commissioners Appointed by General Assembly, 108-109
Commissioners Arrive in Wyoming, 111
Compromise Act, 114
Confirming Law, 114
Congress Acts on Appeal of Settlers, 75, 79-80
Connecticut. Claim to Wyoming, 27-28
  Plans to Defend Claims, 70-71
Delawares, 19, 20, 21-23, 37, 38
Denison, Col. Nathan, 87
Dollar, Spanish Milled. Origin of Term, 33
Dorrance, Lt.-Col. George, 87
Durkee, Capt. John, 47, 53
Durkee, Robert, 80
Easton, Indian and English Conference at, 29-30
Expedition, Pennamite, Under Col. Francis, 47
Ferries of the Susquehanna River, 71-72
Fort Dickinson, 109, 110, 113
Fort Durkee, 46, 51
Fort Jenkins, 82
Fort Ogden, 44, 52-53
Fort Pittston, 84
Fort Shawnee, 84
Fort Stanwix, N. Y., Treaty at, 41
Fort Wilkes-Barre, 83
Fort Wintermoot, 81-82
Fort Wyoming, 59-60, 62
Forts Built, 81-84
Forts Surrender, 88-93
Forty Settlers, 43
Forty-Fort, 82-83

119

INDEX

Franklin, Capt. John, 110-11
French and Indian War, 29-30, 41
Gardner, John, 87
Governor's Proclamation, 1770, 53, 54
Grasshopper War, 22-23
Hacklein, Peter, Sheriff of Northampton Co., 58
Hadsall Family Massacred, 87
Harding Family Massacred, 86-87
Harding Memorial, 87
Hartley, Col., 94
Ice Flood, 1784, 107-108
Indians, Description of Pennsylvania, 17-24
Indians Driven from Wyoming, 38, 102
Indians Return to Valley, 78, 88
Indian Strongholds Broken, 103
Jennings, John, Sheriff, 45
Liquor Sale to Indians Unlawful, 72
Luzerne, Chevalier de la, 113
Luzerne County Established, 113
Massacre, First of Wyoming, 37
Massacre of Wyoming, *see* Wyoming, Battle of
Maughwauwame, 22, 37
Mill Creek Settlement, 35-36
Nanticokes, 19, 23
Ogden, Capt., Pennamite Lessee, 54-55, 58, 61-62
Paris, Treaty of, 41
Patterson, Justice of the Peace, 109-10
Peace, Days of, 63-66
Penn, William. Claim to Wyoming, 27-28
Penn Refuses Appeal of Connecticut, 70-71
Pennamite-Yankee Wars, 27-28, 42-48, 51-56, 58-63, 105-14
Pennamites Outwit Yankees, 44-45
Pennsylvania, Proprietaries of, 21, 22, 28, 41-42, 44, 46, 47, 48, 62, 75
Pennsylvania-Connecticut Controversy Renewed, 105-14
Pennsylvania Claimants, First Occupation of Wyoming, 44
Pennsylvania Lessees Settle in Wyoming, 42
Plunkett's Expedition, 74-76

INDEX

Queen Esther's Rock, 91
Ransom, Samuel, 80
Regimental Companies in Wyoming, 80
Revolutionary War Breaks Out, 72
Settlement of Wyoming, First, 32-38
Settlement of Wyoming, Second, 42
Settlers Come to Valley, Additional, 45
Settlers Join in Revolution, 72-74
Settling Right, Meaning of Term, 65
"Shades of Death," 93
Shawnees, 19, 20-21, 22
Six Nations, 19, 21, 22, 37
Six Nations, Sullivan's March Against, 102-104
Slocum, Frances, 99-102
Stewart, Capt. Lazarus, 51, 56
Stockades Built, 66
Succotash, Origin of Name, 18
Sullivan Expedition, 102-104
Surveyor, First, of Wyoming, 42
Surrender, General Articles of, 91-92
Surrender of Fort Dickinson, 110-11
Surrender of Fort Durkee, 48
Suspension Act of 1788, 114
Susquehanna Company
  Formation at Windham, 32
  Meetings, 34-35, 41-42, 51, 68-69
Susquehanna Company Agent to Confer with Gov. Penn, 63
Susquehanna Purchase, Name of Territory, 35, 38
Susquehanna Purchase at Albany, 34
Teedyuscung, Delaware Chief, 36-37
Townships, Laying Out of, 43
Treaty of Fort Stanwix, N. Y., 41
Treaty of Paris, End of French and Indian War, 41
Trenton, Decision of, 105
Valley Resettled After Massacre, 103
West Branch Settlement, 74
Westmoreland District Meeting, 1776, 78-79
Westmoreland Town Meeting, 72-74
White Man, First to Visit Valley, 26-27

INDEX

Wilkes-Barre, Naming of, 46-47
Wyoming, Meaning of Name, 22
Wyoming, Battle of, 90-93
   Burial of Victims, 95
   Relation to Revolution, 93
Wyoming Monument, 95
Wyoming Settlement, Directors of, 69
Wyoming Settlement, Meeting of Proprietors, 65
Wyoming Valley, Location of, 16
Yankee-Pennamite Wars, *see* Pennamite-Yankee Wars
Yankees Attack Fort Wyoming, 59
Yankees Depart, 1770, 55
Yankees Driven Out of Valley, 45, 48
Yankees Overcome by Pennamites in 1770, 55-56
Yankees Return to Valley, 51, 56
Yankees Surrender to Pennamites, 1771, 59
Zinzendorf, Count Nicholas, 26-27

www.ingramcontent.com/pod-product-compliance
Lightning Source LLC
Chambersburg PA
CBHW060016050426
42448CB00012B/2780